Foreword

The wartime sabotage organization known as Special Operations Executive, which was created in July 1940 in response to the Prime Minister's directive to 'set Europe ablaze', formed a Belgian branch designated T Section in December 1940, initially as an independent offshoot of the French Section. Although much has been written about SOE's clandestine activities elsewhere in Europe, very little has been published about the operations of T Section, which was headed at first by a Coldstream Guards officer, Claude Knight, and later by the couturier Hardy Amies.

One of the reasons for the almost complete dearth of information about Knight's work is the political wrangling that dogged its development while it attempted to liaise with the Belgian government-in-exile, various competing Belgian resistance groups, and Britain's own Secret Intelligence Service which cast a gimlet eye over most of SOE's adventures. The majority of its agents, either dropped by parachute or landed by Lysander aircraft into Nazi-occupied Belgium during the first three years of the War, were captured by the enemy which proved itself to be the master of the dangerous counter-intelligence game which decimated so many networks in France and especially Holland.

After a slow start, T Section parachuted its first agent, Emile Tromme, into his home country in May 1941, but unfortunately he landed in the middle of a prisoner-of-war camp from which he had to escape before he could finally make contact with London four months later. He remained at liberty until October when he was arrested, and was shot in February the following year. This inauspicious beginning set the scene for subsequent missions, since most of those who followed Tromme perished in execution yards, prison cells or concentration camps. By the end of October 1942 T Section had despatched 27 agents and 18 wireless operators to Belgium, but only a lucky 13 had avoided falling into German hands. Worse still, neither Knight nor his staff at SOE headquarters had the slightest clue that the majority of their radio circuits were being run under the enemy's control.

It is against this background of disaster and deception that Jacques Doneux was parachuted into Belgium in August 1943, accompanied by the man he calls Paul, Captain A.J. Wendelen, who had only recently returned from an assignment lasting an astonishing 16 months. Incredibly, both men survived their harrowing experiences and eventually made their way back to England. Wendelen was injured when he made a bad parachute landing, and Doneux was obliged to extend his mission, which had not been planned to last not more than a few months, until June 1944 when he was flown home from Gibraltar, having endured appalling hardship on his journey across Europe. Doneux escaped with his life, but with the loss of some of his toes to frostbite, while Wendelen was one of seventeen agents to undertake two missions, and one of only three to survive a third. SOE's statistics speak for themselves. Of 163 agents despatched to Belgium, 93 were either arrested or killed, a rate of attrition suffered only by RAF Bomber Command aircrew flying over the Reich.

Doneux's account, originally published in 1956, remains the only first-hand account of a T Section mission into Belgium, and is regarded as authentic in every detail. The author discreetly omits any description of the political intrigues in London, or the inter-agency rivalries that might have prevented the Germans from taking such a toll from the *résistants*, but what emerges is a story of breathtaking courage, personal suffering, and an impressive commitment to a cause that at times must have seemed hopeless. Despite his poor condition after his escape over the Pyrenees, and his prolonged hospitalisation in Spain, Doneux survived until 1971 and leaves us with this inspiring record of one of T Section's successes.

Nigel West

THEY ARRIVED BY MOONLIGHT

THEY ARRIVED BY MOONLIGHT

CAPT. JACQUES DONEUX

ST ERMIN'S
PRESS

A *St Ermin's Press* Book

Published by St Ermin's Press in 2000
in association with Little, Brown & Company

Reprinted 2001

Introduction copyright © Westintel Research Ltd
Copyright © Jacques Doneux and St Ermin's Press

A CIP catalogue record for this book is available from the British Library.

ISBN: 1 903608 00 7

Typeset by Palimpsest Book Production Limited,
Polmont, Stirlingshire
Printed and bound in Great Britain
by Clays Ltd, St Ives plc

St Ermin's Press
In association with
Little, Brown and Company (UK)
Brettenham House
Lancaster Place
London WC2E 7EN

Contents

CHAPTER 1

Landing

It was 9 o'clock on 11 August 1943. On the darkened airstrip the motors of the Halifax revved, caught and rose to a full and powerful roar. The plane inched forward, taxied to the end of its runway, turned and began to pick up speed. In a few seconds we were airborne. It had begun. Somewhere in Belgium a small field was waiting for us to drop by moonlight.

Paul and I, trussed up in our parachute harnesses, were half sitting, half lying on something we thought might be a rubber dinghy, inside the aircraft. A small white bulb glowed in the ceiling, but apart from this the plane was in darkness. The dispatchers – the men who would see us safely out when the time came to jump – were forward in the nose of the aircraft. Paul and I were alone. I do not remember that we said anything to each other.

We climbed steadily. There was a small window in the side of the fuselage and through it we could see the last of the daylight fading; already the moon, about a quarter full, was quite clear to the eye. After a while one of the dispatchers came through into the cabin.

'All right?' he asked.

We nodded.

'Better make sure,' he went on. 'After we cross the coast you won't be able to see a damned thing in 'ere. Pitch, it'll be. All the lights go out then.'

'Whereabouts will we cross it?' I asked.

'Bournemouth area.'

My wife was in Bournemouth.

The dispatcher came and squatted down near us. There was a silence. The light in the roof of the cabin winked undramatically and went out. Very shortly the silence was broken by the angry clatter of enemy flak. The plane ducked away from it and we resumed our course, the flak still reaching up for us in the night. I glanced at the dispatcher and he noticed I was looking at him.

'That's nothing,' he said reassuringly. 'You should hear 'em on Fridays.'

Paul and I had a long pull at the hot coffee, generously laced with rum, which they had provided for us before we took off. Then we tried to lie down and get some sleep. The heaters had been turned on and it was getting very hot; we were so tightly strapped that we could scarcely move and we wore full civilian clothing under our flying suits.

I must have fallen asleep all the same, for when I next looked at my watch it was 11.30. I glanced through the window and saw that we were flying very low. Threads of cloud blew past every now and then. Paul was still asleep, but presently the two dispatchers came and woke him. We had about twenty minutes. They checked our parachute harnesses, then dragged out two packages and put them ready near the aperture. These packages were sizeable and contained all the equipment Paul and I were taking with us. Once they were in position, the dispatchers opened the aperture and the cold night air burst in. We were not sorry to feel it. One of the men plugged in the intercom, and the Captain's voice came through.

'Only a few miles to go, boys,' he said. 'Bit of a snag though; this cloud means we can't be sure of finding your exact field. Do you want to drop somewhere roughly in the neighbourhood or would you rather scrub round this and try again another day?'

I looked at Paul. He had chosen this particular area, since it was one he had used before. As it was my first trip into Occupied Europe I thought it best to leave the decision to him. He was not long in taking it.

'We'll risk it,' he said. 'As long as we're somewhere in the district I shall know the way.'

'Right-ho,' called the Captain. 'Ready to go when I give the word. Soon as we're over an open bit with no trees or houses. Number two to follow as quickly as poss.'

I was to be the first man out. The dispatchers fastened our static lines and then those on our packages' chutes. I took up my position on the very edge of the aperture. One of the dispatchers gave me a thumbs-up; then, smiling, he took his false teeth out and put them in his pocket.

'We don't want 'em to shoot out the hole when I give you the word "go",' he explained. 'They might bite you when you land!'

Normally we used a light as signal to jump, but now, since the decision would have to be taken quickly, the Captain would tell the dispatcher over the intercom when the moment had come. The dispatcher would then tell me. Looking down through the aperture I could see nothing but the tops of the scurrying clouds. Once or twice there was a break in them and then, a few hundred feet below, I could see the fields and hedges of Belgium. My legs were already hanging out into space and my hands were gripping the sides of the aperture. The plane bumped and lurched. The Captain told the dispatcher that we should be dropping from about 700 feet. I clung there for about ten minutes as the plane plunged about in the low cloud. Suddenly, the dispatcher put his face down to mine and said: 'GO!'

I stared at him, almost surprised, for a moment; then I lifted myself up on my hands and let myself drop through the opening.

The slipstream nearly knocked the breath out of me. It was bitterly cold: I might just have dived into an icy swimming bath. I seemed to be spinning round as if caught in a whirlpool. My parachute opened but some part of my equipment, probably the large rubber cushion in my seat pocket, must have been projecting and the wind snatched at it and spun me round. The result was that my rigging lines were all twisted. I grabbed hold of the harness straps above my head and pulled them sharply apart; I had to get rid of the twist before I hit the ground and, since we had jumped from only 700 feet, that did not leave much time. At last I spun back and felt the rigging lines untwist themselves. I was all right, but the time I had used sorting out my chute should have been spent, according to training instructions, checking the line of fall and trying to see where Paul – and the packages – were falling. I had no time for this, however, for no sooner did I look down to see where I was landing than I hit something extraordinarily soft. I rolled over in a bundle once or twice and then hit the ground remarkably painlessly. I sat there for a moment and then peered round me to see what I had struck. A large and shaggy haystack stood just to my left. I must have hit the stack and then rolled from it to the ground. My landing was the more lucky since the field where the stack stood was littered with a number of jagged stones.

I could just hear the drone of the departing plane and so could plot roughly the direction in which Paul and our packages should be found. There were clouds in front of the moon, but nevertheless I was able to get some idea of the surrounding countryside. I had landed on the top of a hillock, in a rough field from which the corn had recently been cut. About thirty yards away to the right a dark mass which must have been a hedge dropped down and out of sight behind the crest of the hill. There was no wind, so my parachute had collapsed on landing. Now the plane was no longer audible and the silence was absolute. A few drops of rain were falling.

Our instructions were always to draw our revolvers on landing and slip the safety-catch off so that we would be ready for trouble. Sitting there in the dark field with not a sound to be heard, I felt this precaution somewhat superfluous. Instead I reached into the pocket which contained my whisky flask. I felt much relieved that I had landed safely, and it was several minutes before I realized that there was work to be done. I stood up and started to remove my equipment; gloves, helmet and goggles were the first to go. A jerk at a short piece of cord was enough to release Cuthbert, my pigeon, in his wicker basket; a twist and a blow on the contact box and my parachute harness fell away; a sharp pull on the zips of my jumping suit enabled me to

4

remove that in no time, and there I was: a scruffy little Belgian subject in a rumpled blue serge suit and an equally rumpled raincoat. The only thing out of keeping was the fact that I was wearing army boots. This was not an oversight (no one could have been more carefully checked for incriminating details than an agent about to take off) but a deliberate decision. I had fractured my ankle during training and we were not at all sure that it would stand the strain of a similar bad landing this time. So it was agreed that I should jump in boots, which gave the ankle a certain amount of support, and change into a pair of Belgian shoes as soon as I landed. My shoes were in my package, of course, which made it doubly important to locate it as quickly as possible. I did not want to walk around in a pair of boots stamped 'W.D. 1943' for longer than I could help.

I rolled up my chute and collected my equipment, checking that I had it all; two journeys to the hedge were sufficient to dispose of it in a reasonably safe temporary hiding-place. This accomplished, I set off in the direction I had plotted earlier to look for Paul. I walked along the hedge expecting to see him approaching at any moment, since he would have as good an idea of my location as I had of his. Nothing stirred. I had covered about a hundred yards when I began to feel uneasy, so I picked up two stones and began to chink them together in the manner we had previously agreed; anything, of course, was better than calling out to each other, for voices can carry miles at night-time. There was no answering chink and I must confess to feeling rather foolish standing there in the dark, wet hedgerow, knocking a couple of pebbles together. I gave up and walked on a few yards. The hedge came to an end where a narrow cobbled path slanted across it. The light and the rain were both getting worse and it was difficult to get any clear picture of the topography. There was another largeish field on my right, while away to the left the pathway faded into the murky night. I strained my eyes down this path and saw a dark mass which seemed to be lying across it some forty yards away. When I hurried towards it I found that it was a collapsed parachute; just beyond I found Paul, flat on his back, his arms and legs flung out.

'Paul,' I whispered.

There was no reply. I knelt beside him. To my relief he opened his eyes and looked vacantly about him.

'Are you all right?' I asked.

He smiled, but did not reply. I tried to remember the first aid we had been taught. The most important thing was to find out if he had broken anything.

'Try to move your feet,' I whispered. He did so. 'Now your arms,' I said. He managed this too. From what I could recall, this meant that he had not broken either his neck or his back; in the latter case he would not have been able to move his legs, in the former, the same would apply to his arms. At least, I thought this was so.

With my help he sat up, and I put the whisky flask to his lips. This revived him sufficiently to be able to tell me what had happened. He too had had a twist when he left the plane and, like myself, had only just had time to clear it when he hit the ground; unlike me, however, he had landed not on the soft roof of a haystack but flat on his back on the cobbled path where I had found him. All the breath was knocked out of him.

It is often thought that a descent by parachute is like floating down onto a feather mattress, but this is far from true; in fact the impact when you hit the earth is equivalent to a jump from 15 feet. Normally, of course, you are prepared for the landing and are able to break your fall; in Paul's case, however, this had not been possible owing to the twist in his chute. It was as if he had fallen from a second-floor window and landed flat on his back in the roadway. In the circumstances we were lucky to find that, though he was in great pain, he had not broken anything. I was the more pleased since had he been too badly injured to move, I should have been forced to leave him where he was. There was no such thing as the team spirit in our business; or if there was, it was the kind which demanded that no individual misfortune should be allowed to interfere with the plans of the Organization. Sentiment was forbidden by orders.

I helped Paul out of his flying equipment (as he was a shortish

6

fellow this was not too difficult) and he took another pull at the whisky. He shook his head and then, with an effort, struggled to his feet and limped over to the hedge which was soaked with rain. Paul fell rather than walked through the hedge and I followed. We found that a small cart track led up towards a thick copse whose jagged outline stood out black against the dark bruise of the sky. I helped Paul along the path and into the copse; there we found a small clearing which, under the umbrella of the trees, was not too damp. I left him there and went back to collect the equipment. Several trips were needed and when it was all in the copse we checked it through to make sure that we had left nothing behind. This was a drill we had often followed during training.

The rain hissed steadily in the trees. I made a half-hearted attempt to locate our two packages (I still had my W.D. boots on) but soon desisted. I could not have found them now if they had been only a few yards away, so dark had it become. We unrolled the bandages which we had bound round our ankles before take-off and buried them in the floor of the copse, then rolled ourselves in our parachutes and tried to get some sleep.

I had a cigarette first, one of the Belgian ones I had been given, a wretched little tube of black cardboard. I also found my glasses which I had put in one of the pockets of my flying suit and I had my revolver, as did Paul, ready for use. We put our two pigeons, still in their containers, under some nearby bushes. The weather improved during the night. By 4 o'clock the rain had stopped and, waking from one of my short dozes, I could see the stars through the roof of the copse. The parachute silk was warm and the temperature quite mild so that sleep was not altogether impossible, nor was I unbearably cramped when I awoke.

About dawn I gave up the effort to sleep any more and slipped away from the clearing to have a cigarette. There was a fairly thick ground mist and the trees dripped silently in the damp air. I was just stamping out my cigarette when Paul called to me. He was very stiff after his sleep and it was agony for him to stand, but he did so and even achieved a few steps as I watched apprehensively. The sun was rising now and the greyness of the scene was alleviated by the clear blue of the sky. Somewhere a bird was singing. The mist was thinning and soon it would be full day.

I went back to make sure that we had left no traces of our arrival and again checked the line of flight of our plane; this was vital if we were to find our packages. Then I returned to the copse where I had left Paul and together we buried our kit in the thick undergrowth.

We walked to the edge of the copse and saw that we were about 300 yards from a roof visible a little farther down the hill. We approached warily and found it to be a barn. There was no one about and it appeared to be quite deserted. It was a matter of more than incidental interest to us to know where we were in relation to our planned dropping point, for that point had been only a few miles from the French frontier and it was by no means certain that we were not now in France. Since we had only Belgian papers it was imperative to get our bearings as painlessly as possible. But more important still was to find our packages; my W.D. boots weighed on my mind as much as they did on my feet. Our hands on our guns, we began the search.

Ahead of us, in the line of flight which I had plotted, the ground fell away to a shallow valley and then, half a mile farther on, rose in a gentle slope to a height of perhaps a hundred feet. The whole landscape was interspersed with clumps of small trees, leafy bushes and shaggy undergrowth in which our packages might well lie hidden. Anyone who has looked for a golf ball on a particularly sporting course will know the kind of search with which we were faced. We started the usual procedure; fanning out, we walked in ever-increasing circles. I pressed forward while Paul, moving only with the greatest difficulty, stayed nearer the landing point. I felt very conspicuous and, after an hour had passed with no success, considerably agitated. By this time I had reached the top of the hill on the far side of the valley. Beyond it was another identical to it, while the track along which I had been walking with what nonchalance I could assume, ended a few hundred yards ahead in some thick woods. I despaired of searching there and returned to see what Paul thought.

'What time do you make it?' he asked.

I looked at my watch, a Swiss one which was standard issue on these trips.

'Eight o'clock,' I replied.

'We daren't hang about here much longer,' Paul decided. 'Either they haven't dropped the stuff or they dumped it a long way from here. Anyway there's no sense in going on looking indefinitely, and if the Boches have come across any of it they'll be on to us in no time.'

I nodded. Lone planes were suspect with the Germans in any case, though the usual thing was to camouflage the purpose of the flight by dropping leaflets somewhere along the line. If the packages were found, however, this mild deception would quickly be exploded and the area would be cordoned off and ourselves trapped. Our best course was to quit the neighbourhood and then, if possible, to discover exactly what neighbourhood it was.

We returned to the copse where we had left the pigeons and took them out from the bushes where I had hidden them. We had been told that if we released them within a few hours of our arrival it would be better not to feed them, since the lack of food would be an added incentive for them to return home with all speed. On the other hand, they must be watered, since the heat in the plane and their long confinement was bound to make them thirsty, and while they would go home for food they would not be so nostalgic in their quest for water and might come down as soon as they saw some.

I opened my pigeon's container and, holding the creature by the back, with his wings pinioned against it, I lifted him out. This was a delicate manoeuvre, for the birds are so sensitive that to damage one feather might well ruin his chances of getting home. While I held the bird against my body, Paul reached into the container and removed the small water and grain bottles which were packed inside it.

'Just the water,' I said.

Paul took the cap off the water bottle and looked inside. With a sudden movement he turned the bottle upside down.

'Paul,' I cried. 'What the—?'

But as I looked I realized why he had done it. No water poured to the ground. The bottle had been empty all the time; they had never bothered to fill it. We put the pigeon back in its container and opened the other one, but found only two more empty bottles. During our hunt for the packages we had covered the surrounding district pretty well and had not come across any sign of rivers, brooks or even puddles. The rain of the previous night had soaked in and disappeared.

'What about this?' I asked, bringing out my whisky flask. It was the only liquid we had. The joke was a poor one, but it was the only means we had of relieving our feelings about the man who had failed to fill the water bottles. All we could do now was to send the pigeons off and hope for the best. We took the message pads from the containers and I wrote out the following message:

TIBALT AND HILLCAT ARRIVED SAFELY BUT HAVE NO IDEA WHERE WE ARE. WILL CONTACT THE NATIVES. NO SIGN OF OUR PACKAGES. PLEASE SEND NEWS BY B.B.C.

I carefully folded the thin paper, rolled it up and put it in the small tube which fitted to the bird's leg. I copied the message on Paul's paper and we attached the two cylinders to our birds' legs. Then we carried them to open ground and released them simultaneously. They flapped for a moment, then they began to climb, circling higher and higher into the clear morning sky. Together they headed into the west and soon they were lost to sight. As it turned out, neither of them ever reached England; Paul's was never seen again, mine was found dying in a wood near Liège by a member of the Resistance. As a result the message reached London by an overland route nearly two months after I had written it, by which time I myself had made contact.

'What now?' I asked Paul as we turned away after releasing the pigeons.

'We must find out where we are,' he replied.

We walked back to the cross-road which I had seen during my quest for the packages; I had not actually been right up to it and we hoped to find a signpost to give us some idea of our bearings. Disappointed, we tossed up to decide which way to go and, in the event, turned left. The road dipped and twisted between green hedges, and after a quarter of an hour's walk we saw, down to our left, a hamlet consisting of a few farm cottages and a small church. So far we had not met a soul but now, as we walked boldly into the village, we were met with suspicious looks from the farmers and peasant women whose ducks and chickens we scattered in our path. We were dressed in city clothes and our incongruousness must have led them to imagine that we were agricultural inspectors or even Gestapo men. Since most country people had some livestock or something of the kind hidden away in their cellars or backyards, such strangers could scarcely expect a ready welcome.

As we passed the first houses, we saw a priest come out of the church and go into the little presbytery which faced it. He seemed the best source of information and accordingly we went and knocked on the presbytery door. It was not opened; instead an old woman appeared at a first-floor window and asked us what we wanted.

'May we speak a few words with Monsieur le Curé?' asked Paul.

The old woman glowered suspiciously, her suspicion evidently not unmingled with fear.

'He has just said Holy Mass,' she answered, 'and is having his breakfast. He can't see anyone.'

'For a few minutes only,' Paul promised.

The old woman slammed the window shut without a word. Paul and I looked at each other and shrugged. We were about to turn away when the door was opened a few inches by the priest himself; he was a very old man and seemed very frightened and uncertain.

'What do you want to see me for?' he asked.

'For patriotic reasons,' Paul replied.

The priest looked more frightened than ever as his hand gripped

11

the door for support. It was easy to be impatient with him, but his terror was understandable; there was nothing to show that we were not *agents provocateurs*. It was my first experience of the fear that each man felt towards his fellows in Occupied Europe. A continent was divided against itself and no one who lived in it felt safe with his neighbour.

'What is it you want?' the old man asked once more.

There was no sense in being anything but direct, since to hedge would only be to terrify the priest still further.

'We have just arrived,' Paul told him, 'and we want to know where we are.'

'In Belgium,' muttered the old man, as if to mutter were not to have spoken. 'This is Lavaux Ste Anne.'

'Thank you, *mon père*,' Paul said. 'If you are questioned about us, please say that we asked the way of you but that otherwise you know nothing of us.'

The old priest nodded and, giving us his blessing, he closed the door. We walked on through the hamlet and once we were out of sight of it we sat down by a haystack and took out our map. Paul was in great pain and was glad of the rest. We soon found where we were: about four kilometres from La Ferme Physic, the destination we were heading for. This farm was one which Paul knew from his previous trip and where we knew we would be welcomed. The nearest railway station was at Pondrome, some six kilometres distant, but we decided to head for the farm since Paul was now in such pain that he could not face the thought of so long a walk followed by several hours in the train to Brussels. Were we to make the journey to Brussels it would be possible to meet the Count, our contact there, that morning, but as it was we decided to rendezvous with him later in the week and, in the meantime, let Paul recuperate at the farm.

Accordingly, we set off across country towards La Ferme Physic. The journey of four kilometres took us four hours. The rough ground was very difficult for Paul to negotiate and his bruise was beginning to come out; it seemed to cover the whole of his back, and when I looked at it I could imagine what he was suffering, for it was purple and black and soft like a prune. We chose the cross-country route in order to avoid meeting anyone on the road; as a result we met only a couple of peasants, neither of whom paid us any attention, during the whole trip.

'The worst thing is not finding the packages,' Paul said as he struggled along beside me. 'Fine wireless operator you'll be with no set to use.'

'Perhaps we'll hear something from the B.B.C.,' I suggested. Paul did not reply; gritting his teeth, he marched stolidly forward towards La Ferme. Sometime in the early afternoon we reached the place where, if everything had gone to schedule, we should have been dropped. Soon Paul began to recognize various landmarks, but since we were entering the area from an unusual direction it was not easy for him to be sure exactly where the farm was. I was helping him down a steep path which ducked into a thick wood when we caught sight of a rooftop through the trees. We flopped into the thick undergrowth and crept through it towards the house. As soon as we could see it more clearly all Paul's doubts were dispelled.

'This is the place all right,' he whispered.

The farmhouse was a largeish, whitewashed building with a red-tiled roof; near it were various outhouses and sheds. A rusty harrow was leaning against a barn door. As we watched, a woman of about thirty came out of the house. She seemed a cheery person and was singing to herself as she tipped the bucket of scraps she was carrying onto the farmyard floor; hens and ducks came scurrying up at the sight of her and the food.

'The farmer's wife,' Paul said. 'At least I think she is.'

As Paul spoke, a man came out of the farmhouse; there could be no doubt that this was the farmer, and Paul recognized him at once. He was a tall man, broad-shouldered and powerfully built, while his skin was burnished to that deep redness which only country life can bestow upon it. He was in shirt-sleeves and had a battered straw hat on his head. Paul stood up as soon as he saw him, I too rose from our hiding place and together we walked towards the house. They both saw us at the same time. She put down her pail and went over and stood by her husband. I was somewhat uneasy, but Paul pressed forward, and when we were a few yards away he shouted out:

'*Alors*, Guillaume, so you don't remember me?'

The farmer peered at Paul and then exclaimed, 'The Cardinal! The Cardinal! It's the Cardinal!' He rushed up to Paul, grabbed his hand, and swung it up and down vigorously.

'So you do remember,' Paul smiled.

'Ah, for two years we have wondered about you, whether you were safe and well, haven't we, Marie?'

His wife smiled shyly and came forward to join us. She was evidently very pleased to see Paul again, only a little embarrassed that she had not recognized him earlier. I told them about his accident, and at once we were taken into the house, introduced to the family and made comfortable in the best chairs. There were three or four generations of Guillaume's family living in the farm and I was engaged in conversation by his grandmother, a very old lady indeed. There was never any pretence about who we were and Guillaume announced loudly that we had just come from England.

'Ah,' said grandmother to me, 'from England, eh?'

'That's right,' I said.

'From England,' she repeated. 'And how did you come?'

'By aeroplane,' I told her.

'Aeroplane!' There was a silence. 'But isn't that very expensive?' she enquired.

During our conversation Guillaume had rushed off to the bakery and now he returned with a white loaf; butter and jam were put on the table and we could smell frying bacon and fresh coffee being prepared in the kitchen. We were taken into the parlour for the meal, a room which was never used except on special occasions. We were left alone to eat, but Guillaume came in as we were finishing.

'What are your plans from here?' he asked.

'Paul needs rest,' I told him. 'If it is all right with you, we should like to stay a couple of nights.'

'As long as you wish,' he replied.

'The most serious thing,' Paul put in, 'is that we've lost our packages. They must be found.'

'Jacques and I can look for them tomorrow,' Guillaume said, as if this ensured their being found. 'If we have no success there are some units of the *Armée Secrète* in the area. They will help us.'

'Are there many Boches about?' Paul asked.

Guillaume shrugged. 'There is little activity here. They check the trains occasionally, but as long as your papers are all right they don't bother you much. They are looking only for guns and ammunition, you understand. They don't even bother with black marketeers.'

Although it was only late afternoon, Paul and I were dead tired owing to the poor sleep we had had the previous night. After our meal we went straight to bed in the big brass bedstead which the farmer's wife had prepared for us; two embroidered nightshirts were laid out upon it. It required no effort to get to sleep.

Our first day in Belgium was ended.

CHAPTER 2

Finding Accommodation

The next morning was very fine and warm. Paul was extremely stiff; the bruise on his back being very painful and angry, he had been forced to lie on his stomach all night and had not really been able to relax. It was decided that he should stay in bed all day while Guillaume and I went to look for the packages. Luckily both Paul and I had a fair sum of money on us, for he was frankly pessimistic about our chances of finding them. Nevertheless, Guillaume fitted me out with a coarse linen shirt, some blue cotton trousers and a straw hat similar to his own and, after lunch, we set off on two bicycles to begin our search.

First we went back to the copse where we had spent the night; Guillaume and I collected the flying equipment from where we had hidden it and rolled it all into the two parachutes. Guillaume said he would collect them after dark.

'The best thing now is to go back to the place where I landed,' I said. 'We'd better check the line of flight of the plane again before we start looking.'

We left the bikes in the copse and did as I proposed. We searched the wood which I had seen the previous morning, pushing through bushes and thrusting aside the undergrowth, but it was all in vain. We found nothing. After two hours Guillaume called to me. I walked over to him.

'I am sorry,' he said, 'but I must go back to the farm. There's so much work there just now.'

'I'll stay and keep on looking,' I told him.

Beyond several large fields lay another stretch of woods and it was this area which I particularly wanted to inspect. There were some peasants working in the fields and so I was forced to take a long detour in order to avoid them. My main worry was that the Germans had discovered the packages and might be lying in wait to see if anyone came to get them. It was a risk I had to take.

I zigzagged back and forth across the woods, trying not to miss a single yard of them. It was long and hard work, and after an hour and a half I was near despair; then, in a small clearing, something light brown attracted my attention. In addition, I noticed that the ground was trampled and twigs had been snapped off the trees. The brown object proved to be a big piece of sorbo rubber which had been thrust under a pile of dead leaves. I brushed these aside and found some more sorbo packing and pieces of rope. Eventually I came across the brown canvas in which our packages had been wrapped. They needed a lot of padding to protect them; when they came down, they hit the ground with a considerable bang. There was no sign of the contents of the package but, a few yards away along the path which had been trampled through the woods, I found the wrapping of the other package similarly buried under leaves. Again there was no sign of the contents. The thieves, whoever they were, had been thorough.

I could only return to the place where I had hidden my bike and pedal back to the farm, where I told Paul and Guillaume what I had found.

'It's pretty certain,' Paul said, 'that the Boches didn't find the stuff.'

'They'd have no reason to be in the woods,' agreed Guillaume.

'Have you any idea who could have taken it?' I asked.

'*Réfractaires*, almost certainly,' he replied.

Réfractaires were young men in unreserved occupations who, if they did not hide, would be conscripted by the Germans for forced labour. To avoid this was considered a loyal duty by the Belgians, and the evasion was subsidized from across the Channel.

'Have you any way of getting in touch with them?' Paul demanded.

'Certainly I have, but it may take a few days. They move about and are not easy to get hold of.'

'We can't wait that long,' Paul said. 'I'm all right now and we must get on to Brussels tomorrow. When are the trains?'

'There is a train every afternoon at two o'clock from Pondrome,' Guillaume said, 'but you can never be sure that it will come in on time. One must be patient and hope.'

The whole family turned out to say goodbye to us when the next morning, after an early lunch, we set off for the station. Guillaume was quite indignant when we offered to pay for our stay.

'It's not our money,' Paul protested.

'Use it to fight the Boches,' Guillaume replied.

Paul had made arrangements for Guillaume to notify us if he had any news of the packages and so, with kisses from the women and handshakes from the men, we set off for Pondrome.

Paul was much the better for his day in bed, but all the same he had to sit down and have a rest before we went into the village.

'You go ahead,' he told me. 'It's better if we don't enter the place together.'

I did as he said and, leaving him where he was, I walked through the village. In the courtyard of the flat-faced little station there were some 30–40 German soldiers standing and talking. I had to push through them to get to the booking hall. As I did so I gazed down at my feet, not sure that I could trust myself to look at the Germans without giving something away by my expression, and was reminded that I was still wearing my W.D. boots. They were squeaking too, and I was convinced that everyone had seen them or would do so soon. Actually, no one paid me the slightest attention and I was able to book my ticket without difficulty. I went into the waiting room and sat down.

Paul came in and sat down near me. We ignored each other for a minute or so and then he passed some remark about the state of the railways, or the weather or something, and we got into conversation as strangers (other than English strangers) will do in railway stations.

'As there seems to be no sign of the train we may as well go and have a drink to pass the time,' Paul suggested, after a half-hour had passed.

'Good idea,' I said. 'We'll be able to see it coming from the café.'

Our conversation was suitably stilted for the benefit of anyone who might happen to be listening, and it continued in the same vein as we had our beers. When the train was an hour overdue the crowd in the café began to move over to the station. We followed and a quarter of an hour later the train crept into sight. It was packed, but we contrived to edge our way in and soon we were on our way to Brussels.

We arrived in Brussels four hours late, but we gathered that to be only as late as that was to have made good time. By now it was 8 o'clock at night. There were two German military policemen on the platform but they paid no attention to civilian travellers and we left the station without incident. We walked to the Grand Boulevard and sat down on a bench to discuss our next step. There were a great many German troops about; the private soldiers were rather a scruffy lot in their coarse battle-dress, but the officers, with their well-cut uniforms, silver daggers dangling from their belts and caps high-peaked at the front, were very smart and I could not help staring at them.

'The first thing,' Paul said, 'is to find you somewhere to stay. I've got friends who can put me up, but I can't take you along as well.'

'What's the best thing to do?' I asked.

He did not answer but took out a piece of paper and began to write on it. Trains rattled past us and numerous cyclists pedalled along the boulevard. There were few cars and the majority of them were running on coke boilers and not petrol; even the German army lorries used these boilers.

Paul finished his letter and, sealing it down, handed it to me. He told me the address where I should take it, and added, 'That is my mother's house. I've asked her if she can let you stay for a few days until you find somewhere permanent.'

'Are you sure it will be all right for her?'

'Don't worry,' he said, 'she will help you if she can. But I saw her the last time I was here and I promised her then that I would not come back to Belgium, so don't tell her I'm here. Just say that I gave you the letter immediately before you took off from England.'

'Of course,' I agreed.

'If she can't do anything for you, come back here. I'll wait for half an hour.'

'Right.'

'Otherwise be near this seat every evening between six and six-thirty and I'll be able to contact you.'

I nodded and stood up. We shook hands in the way that is customary on the Continent and I walked to the Rue Bosquet where Paul's mother lived. I found the house easily enough and pulled the bell and waited. I heard it jangle but there was no reply. I tried again and still no one came. After a third tug I was about to give up when an elderly lady came up to me and asked what I wanted.

'I am looking for Madame M——' I told her. She repeated the name, staring at me as she did so. 'That's right,' I said.

She seemed to hesitate and then she said, 'Well, what do you want of me?'

'You are she?'

'I am.'

'May I have a few words with you in private?'

She looked at me suspiciously again and then opened the door of the house and allowed me to go in. As soon as she had closed the door she turned and said, 'Well, what is it you want?'

'I have something for you,' I told her, taking Paul's letter from my pocket and holding it out to her.

'I am expecting no letters,' she said.

'Read it,' I urged.

Still she did not take it.

'Who is it from?'

It was I who hesitated this time and then, pretty sure that there was no one about, I answered, 'It is from your son.'

'No,' she said, cowering away, 'that's impossible. He's – he's not here. He's been away a long time. I don't know where he is. I haven't seen him for years.' She stopped speaking and stood watching me.

'Isn't there somewhere else we could talk?' I enquired gently.

She made no reply, but just stood and stared at the letter which I was still holding out to her.

'Madame,' I said, 'I would not tell you this if there were any other way of convincing you. I have just arrived from England where your son is. He gave me this letter before I left and asked me to send you his love and to tell you that he is safe and well. He has even been awarded the Croix de Guerre for his work in Belgium when he was here.'

Even now her suspicions were not resolved, but so great was her desire to read the letter that she abandoned her fears, grabbed it from my hand and ripped open the envelope. No sooner had she read the letter than she burst into tears, threw her arms about me and kissed me on both cheeks.

'Oh, Monsieur,' she cried, 'how is my Paul? Have you known him for long? He is quite safe, isn't he, Monsieur? He's not doing anything dangerous, is he? Did he get back to England easily? He is all right, isn't he? He's given up the work he was doing as he promised he would, hasn't he?'

I nodded and smiled. All the while Paul was sitting on a bench in the Grand Boulevard not 300 yards away.

'I wonder if you can put me up for a few days,' I enquired bluntly when she had finished re-reading the letter. Time was short and Paul would be gone if I did not hurry.

'I would,' she answered, 'really I would, but I have some people staying and I cannot trust them – paying guests, you know. I am so sorry. I would like so much to help a friend of my Paul's, but – what can I do?'

'It doesn't matter, Madame. There are plenty of places I can go to. I just thought . . .'

Paul was still sitting where I had left him.

'No go?'

'There are people staying,' I told him. 'But she is very well and pleased to have news of you.'

He smiled, then said, 'We still haven't found anywhere for you to stay though.'

We swung aboard a passing tram and soon after 9.30 we rang the bell of a flat in a small side street off the Avenue Louise, near Gestapo headquarters. There was no one in. As we came out of the flats we saw a man coming towards us down the street. He seemed a harmless character, so Paul stopped and asked him what time curfew was.

'How come you don't know?' he asked in a surly manner.

'We're new in Brussels,' Paul explained. 'We're from Liège.'

'Well, it's eleven o'clock,' the man said. It seemed he was just being cussed, for he evinced no further interest in us but shambled off down the street.

'We must hurry,' said Paul.

We went to another address Paul knew of, but again there was no answer to our ring. It was past 10 o'clock. There were not many trains running now and our next journey, to the Rond Point near the Cinquantenaire, took over 25 minutes. As we hurried through the emptying streets to a large block of modern flats, it was now a quarter to eleven. Paul glanced hurriedly down the list of tenants in the hallway and pressed the button of the one he wanted. We waited anxiously.

Suddenly a voice spoke through the little microphone on the panel. 'Who is it?'

'Le Cardinal.'

A buzzer sounded and we pushed open the now unlocked inner door. The lift was not working and we had to run up the six flights to the flat which we were looking for. As we reached the landing a young woman came out of the flat and beckoned to us to come in. We slipped through the door and went into the sitting-room.

'What are you doing in Brussels?' she asked Paul.

He explained our position and asked if we could stay for two or three nights (it was now too late for him to go back to the place where he had first intended to stay). As we were talking a key turned in the door and a young man came in. For a moment he was quite astonished, then he remembered Paul and shook his hand warmly.

There was very little room in the flat, but we were welcome to make ourselves as comfortable as we could. Food was another problem, since they were going away for the weekend and there was very little in the larder. Paul and I had not eaten since mid-morning, but we had to make do with a few potatoes and some bread and cheese.

'How long are you thinking of staying?' our host asked.

'I'm hoping to find somewhere for Jacques to stay when I see a friend of mine tomorrow,' Paul said, meaning the Count.

'We shall be away until Monday, so you're welcome to remain here a couple of days.'

'It's very kind of you,' I said.

We made up a couple of beds on the floor and, after a good wash, turned in. Next day we woke to the sound of heavy rain plashing in the courtyard. This was the more annoying because the daily woman was coming that morning and would not leave the flat till 4 o'clock; it was necessary for us to be out all that time. Paul was going to see the Count, so I donned my W.D. boots (which were less glossy than they had been but still a formidable size) and set off on a shopping expedition.

I walked to the centre of the city and found a shop in the Rue Haute which stocked toilet articles, the things I most needed. It was the first shop I had been into and I was slightly nervous; though I knew Belgium pretty well and, of course, spoke perfect French, I had usually been the guest of friends or relatives on my trips before the War and had never had much call to go into shops and buy things myself.

I walked into the shop as boldly as I might and asked, first of all, for a razor.

'Certainly, sir,' said the assistant, 'what kind would you like?'

'Oh,' I said, 'er . . . well, perhaps you could – er – recommend me a good cheap one, could you?'

He put several on the counter and I chose one of them.

'Blades, sir?'

'Please.'

'How many would you like?'

Apparently there is little choice of blades, I thought. 'Oh,' I said, 'a dozen.'

He looked up. 'A dozen, sir? But we never have dozens; fives or tens, yes, but dozens never.'

'Of course, I meant ten,' I said. I thought at the time that I had made a serious bloomer and confused Belgium with England, but I have since realized that even in England razor-blades are always sold in packets of five or ten, so perhaps the mistake was less serious than I thought. I was just being absent-minded.

'I'd like some toothpaste and a toothbrush,' I went on hurriedly.

He offered me a stick of wood with a few bits of bristle stuck in it; in England one would have thrown it out. I made no objection, however.

'Anything else, sir?'

'A face flannel, please,' I said.

'Face flannel? I haven't seen a face flannel in two years.'

'It's the same story everywhere,' I sighed. 'What about shaving soap?'

'You have your coupons, I take it?'

I took out my wallet and thumbed through its contents.

'I seem to have left them at home,' I told him.

He winked. I winked back (it seemed the right thing to do) and he produced a stick of shaving soap and pushed it into my pocket. The same thing happened when I asked for a cake of soap and a soap-box.

'How much is all that?' I asked when he had given me a pair of nail scissors as well.

He glanced round the shop furtively and then whispered, 'You didn't have any coupons, did you?' I shook my head. 'You couldn't produce an empty toothpaste tube, could you?' Again I shook my head. He looked me coolly in the eye and said, 'Five hundred and twenty-five francs.'

I took out my wallet once more, staggered at the price he had asked, and counted out the notes. I passed them to him with another wink and hurried out of the shop. My few purchases had cost more than £2.10s.

The rain was still coming down, but all the same there were a large number of street traders in the Rue Haute and I was offered butter, eggs and liver, and woollen goods, and even an elastic belt at something over £4. One man stopped me and waved a comb in my face; I realized that I had forgotten to buy one.

'How much?' I asked.

'One hundred and fifty francs.'

'I'll give you a hundred,' I said.

Without a word he handed me the comb. It was now early afternoon and I was very hungry, having had no proper meal since leaving La Ferme Physic. I had no idea how to set about getting a meal in a restaurant, however, and did not know whether one had to produce *timbres* or not. I looked in the doors of several small restaurants but, though very tempted to do so, I dared not risk going in.

I still had two hours to kill before I could return to the flat with safety. The rain was falling steadily and my hair hung down, streaming, over my face, while my old shabby mackintosh let in the water with the greatest facility. Only my feet were really dry; I was still wearing my W.D. boots. I wandered around the cold grey city, feeling very homesick and sorry for myself, before eventually walking back to the flat. By now I was absolutely famished.

'Ah,' said Madame, 'I'm just on my way. I'm glad I saw you before I went because now I can give you the key.'

'Thank you,' I said, hanging my sopping raincoat in the vestibule.

'Well, goodbye,' she said, picking up her suitcase.

I could not wait for her to get out of the door so that I could inspect the larder.

'Goodbye,' I said, 'and thank you.'

She left. I hurried into the kitchen and opened every cupboard in the place, but they were all empty of food. In a bin under the sink I found one mouldy potato. I filled a saucepan with water from the tap and put it on the gas stove. When I turned on the tap and applied a match to the ring, there was a little blue 'pop' and then silence: there was no pressure. I had to eat my bad potato raw.

After my 'meal', I went into the sitting room and peeled off the rest of my wet clothes. An hour or so later there was a knock on the door. It was Paul.

'Well,' he cried, 'everything all right?' His arms were full of parcels which he flung onto the sofa. 'I've brought a few provisions and things.'

'Thank God,' I said, 'I'm starving.'

Not only was there food, but he had brought me some cigarettes and a pair of shoes as well.

'I saw the Count,' he told me, as I prepared some food for us, 'and he's found you a place to live. I've got somewhere as well. The Count took me to see a doctor pal of his about my back.'

'What did he say?'

'He told me to rest or something. Important thing is that it's only bruised.'

'That is good news,' I said.

'And how do you like Brussels?'

'Brussels is all right,' I replied, 'but how does one eat in it?'

'It's not so difficult,' he laughed. 'Actually you don't have to worry about *timbres* because if you haven't got any they can charge you more for your meal. Just march in boldly and sit down.'

'I wish I'd known that four hours ago,' I said.

26

CHAPTER 3

A Hurried Departure

The Count called at the flat the next morning. The name suited him because he looked so much as one would expect a Count to look. He was a tall, thin person with chilling grey eyes and a fine aquiline nose.

He took us out to lunch at a small restaurant nearby. The food was of a high standard, and one might have been in the Brussels of pre-war days were it not for the fact that the bill came to something like £5 a head.

As we were smoking our cigarettes after coffee, the Count told us that Jules, his wireless operator, had been able to send a message to London telling them of our safe arrival and of the loss of my sets.

'It seems unlikely, however,' he continued, 'that any delivery can be expected during the present moon period. Only a few days remain and, in any case, we have no receiving ground and no reception committee.'

'That's something we've got to think about as soon as possible,' Paul said. 'We must be ready for the September period.'

'Jules can cope with radio traffic for the moment,' the Count said. 'There's very little just now.'

'Good.'

'Incidentally,' the Count went on, 'about your temporary home.'

'Yes?' I said.

'I've found you two attic rooms in one of the poorer quarters. The people are called Léon. You'll have to pay them three thousand francs a month. It's a lot, but they are taking a great risk and we must compensate them for it. They are both over seventy and you can trust them. I've told them that you are a *réfractaire*, so they know they'll have to be discreet.'

'It sounds perfect,' I said.

'You won't have to register that you're staying there. I've squared things with the local gendarme.'

'You seem to have thought of everything,' I said.

'It's my habit,' he replied, solemnly.

I blushed. 'Oh,' I stammered, 'I didn't mean . . .'

Suddenly both the Count and Paul burst out laughing and I realized that I was having my leg pulled. The Count was able to keep his face so straight that though this was the first time he caught me out it would certainly not be the last.

Paul and the Count had a meeting to attend so I left them in the restaurant and walked back to the flat. Before I left the Count handed me a fat wad of notes which would take care of the rent at the Léons and also serve to keep me comfortably fed on the black market.

The hot tap in the bathroom at the flat was running quite warm for a change, so I took a bath. Before we left England every single thing we were taking with us had been checked through to make sure that there was no trace of English origins left on it, so when I came to make use of my purchases of the previous day, I was considerably amused to find that the razor was stamped 'Made in U.S.A.' and the soap-box actually bore the legend 'Made in England.'

After my bath, having the whole day before me, I decided to wash my underclothes and my shirt. Half an hour later I had festooned the bathroom with my soaking clothes and, arraying myself in a borrowed dressing-gown, left them there to dry. I found an iron in a cupboard and managed to put a crease in my trousers and eliminate the limp-sack look from my raincoat. This done, I decided to get into bed and wait for my things to dry. I lay back under the eiderdown and lit a cigarette. Almost at once, however, I was disturbed by a ring at the downstairs bell. I lifted the speaking tube and asked who was there.

It was Paul. 'Let me in,' he said, 'and hurry.'

I pressed the buzzer to unlock the inner door and in a few seconds Paul burst into the flat.

'What the hell are you doing in a dressing-gown?' he cried.

'Well,' I said, 'my things are drying.'

'Get dressed double quick,' he said. 'We're leaving this flat at once.'

'But that's impossible,' I complained. 'I've got nothing to put on.'

'Don't argue,' Paul said. 'Get your clothes on.'

There was not even time to run the iron over my wet things. Paul dashed around the flat, emptying ashtrays and smoothing out rumpled bedclothes and sofa covers. Meanwhile, I drew on my soaking garments.

'What's all this about?' I asked.

'They're coming back this afternoon. Change of plans. And they're bringing some people with them; they mustn't know we've been here.'

'But what am I going to do?'

'The Count'll take you to the Léons at five-thirty.'

Five minutes later we scuttled out of the flat. Once we were safely in the road, Paul told me where to meet the Count.

'I'll be in touch with you at the Léons as soon as I can,' he finished. 'Now I've got to hurry to a meeting. I'm late already.'

'All right,' I said, shivering.

He left me and hurried away down the street. I stood there, trying to keep my skin from coming into contact with my clammy under-clothes. It was a futile endeavour, so I decided to take a brisk walk instead; I marched up and down the hilly streets of Brussels and ended up near the Parc de Bruxelles. By this time I was perspiring so freely that the beneficial effects of my exercise were quite offset.

At 5 o'clock I boarded a tram (it was a number 58, I remember) which ran along the Avenue Fonsny towards the Pont de Luttre where it turned right into the Avenue du Pont de Luttre. Paul had told me to get off at the first stop after passing under a bridge. I did so, and soon found the turning I was seeking. As I walked up the road I saw two men ahead of me, one of whom was the Count.

29

'Good afternoon,' I said, shaking hands with him.

'Oh, Armand,' he said to his companion, 'this is Michel.'

I shook hands with Armand. It was quite common in our work to be introduced under a variety of names; I think that I had twenty or so different names by the time I was finished.

'Armand can get you anything you need on the black market,' the Count explained. 'I suggest you meet tomorrow and tell him what you want.'

'That would suit me splendidly,' I said.

'Ten-thirty in the Parc Duden?' suggested Armand.

'Perfect.'

We fixed the spot and Armand left us.

'Now then,' said the Count, 'I'll take you to your lodgings.' He led me through some rather shabby side streets and then turned down a cul-de-sac with terraced houses on either side of it. The street petered out into a crumbly patch of unfinished surfacing; a thin fence of clap-board bracketed off the end of it.

'This is the one,' the Count said, ringing the bell of the last house on the left.

The door opened and an elderly woman, small and slight with dry, greying hair, appeared.

'Good afternoon, Madame Léon,' said the Count.

'Monsieur Nulli,' she replied. 'I was expecting you.'

'This is Monsieur Felix,' said the Count, 'your new lodger.'

'You'd better come in,' she told us, looking at me inquisitively.

We went through a narrow vestibule into the kitchen at the back of the house, where Monsieur Léon rose from a black cane chair by the fireside.

'You are very welcome, Monsieur Felix,' he said when we had been introduced. 'I hope you'll treat our home as your own.'

The Count left me with the Léons. Like Paul, he always seemed to have innumerable appointments. Madame Léon had not yet said very much and still looked at me with some suspicion; I imagine it was not so much that she suspected I was engaged on subversive work but rather she feared, as did all Belgians who were sheltering people, that I might be in the pay of the Germans.

'Would it be a good idea, do you think,' I asked, 'if I paid a month's rent in advance?'

This seemed to please the old lady, for she smiled for the first time and said, 'That would be very helpful.' I took out my wallet. 'Monsieur Felix,' she went on, 'will you be taking meals here?'

'I should like to have most of them here, please,' I replied.

'I keep rabbits in the back,' explained the old man, 'so you can be sure of one good meal a week.'

'Would it be a good idea if I gave you something extra so that you can get some more food for me each week?'

'Things *are* very expensive,' Madame Léon murmured.

It was arranged that they should buy white bread, milk and vegetables for the three of us every week. It seemed safer to avoid the jealousy of the old people by getting enough for all of us and, in any case, I saw no reason why they should not profit as much as they could from my presence. I said I would see that we were not without butter, fats, eggs and coffee. Madame warmed to me after this and took me upstairs to see my rooms. Now that we were friends, she forsook her earlier silence for a continual flow of chatter.

'The postman and his wife live here,' she told me as we reached the first landing. 'She's a very nice person, but of course she has the most terrible rheumatism and suffers great pain. Both of them are quite all right,' she finished, nodding meaningly.

On the second landing there was a small sink with a cold tap. The whole of this floor was mine. There were two rooms, a small sitting-room and a bedroom, floored with lino and very cheaply furnished. In the sitting-room there was a plain desk with a wooden chair before it and a couple of armchairs. An iron stove stood out from the wall and a fat flue drew away the smoke and disappeared through the ceiling. There were two allegorical oleographs on the wall, funnily enough both of them English, one of them depicting 'Going with the stream' and the other 'Going against the stream'.

Skimpy curtains hung against the windows.

'Is it all right, Monsieur?' asked Madame.

'It will suit me perfectly,' I said.

She left me to unpack, saying that supper would be at 7 o'clock. When she had gone, I inspected the landing carefully. There was a third door at the back of the house and when I opened it I found myself in a tiny attic room which was used to store firewood. It was lit from a skylight in the roof. I was glad to see that, if need be, I could get out on to the roof and thence on to the rooftops of the adjacent houses. My bedroom was quite bare, containing only a flimsy wooden wardrobe, a brass-headed bed, a small chest of drawers and a marble-topped washstand with a cracked ewer on the top. I made sure that the key turned silently in the bedroom door.

I went back into the sitting-room, looking for somewhere to hide my microphotographs of the codes I would be using as soon as I had a wireless set. The room was so bare that I decided it would have to wait until I had some tools with which to construct a hiding-place. I sat down at the desk, opened my writing case and set about writing out a list of my requirements for when I met Armand in the morning. The most important thing was a supply of squared paper which was vital to the encoding and the decoding of messages.

At 7 o'clock I went down to the kitchen for supper. The postman and his wife had their own kitchen so I was alone with the Léons, a circumstance which I welcomed. The fewer people who saw me frequently the better; I could stand curiosity better than examination. Supper consisted of dark grey and very doughy bread, a little apple sauce to spread on it and a cup of ersatz coffee. During the meal, Madame unleashed her full store of anecdotes and gossip about her neighbours. Her husband hardly said a word. Clearly they were excellently suited.

Afterwards I took out my cigarettes and Monsieur Léon began to fill his pipe.

'How do you manage for tobacco?' I asked.

He was about to speak when his wife answered for him.

'It's almost impossible,' she said. 'He has a ration card, you know, which allows a little each month, but the tobacconists – the tobacconists know which side their bread is buttered.' She made an expressive gesture. 'They never have any for ration, you understand, but if one pays . . .'

'Well, what do you do?'

'I was about to say. A few weeks ago Henri gave up. He came back from the tobacconist and threw all his pipes on the fire.'

'All of them?' I enquired.

'I was just going to tell you. He threw all of them in the fire, then a few days later he came home with a pinch of tobacco someone gave him and so he had to buy a pipe to smoke it in. When that was finished he tried nettle leaves.'

'Nettle leaves?' I said, drawing rather embarrassedly on my cigarette.

'One moment. He dried them in the oven and he's been smoking them ever since.'

I pulled my packet of cigarettes from my pocket and took two or three from it. I held them out to Monsieur Léon and said, 'Please, Monsieur, do smoke these. I am lucky enough to have some more.'

'Oh, no, really. Thank you but—'

'I insist,' I said.

He could hardly believe his good fortune when at last I prevailed upon him to take them and he broke them open and, tapping out his pipe, refilled it with real tobacco.

'It's too kind of you, Monsieur,' said his wife. 'Of course if only I could get some chocolates . . .'

CHAPTER 4

Getting Around

After breakfast – which was exactly the same as the supper of the previous evening – I set out for the Parc Duden. Armand was sitting on a bench waiting for me and, as I approached, motioned me to come and join him.

'Paul told me to tell you that there is news from your farmer friend,' Armand said. 'Your luggage was found by some of the men in the woods apparently, but they won't give it back except for your personal belongings.'

'It hardly seems worth bothering about them,' I mumbled. After all, I had a pair of shoes now.

'Quite. There is only a suitcase and two or three concrete blocks which you must have used as ballast. I don't know why Paul is so determined to fetch them.'

This quite changed the picture. The concrete blocks were very far from being merely ballast: they were camouflage which hid my second set. It was certainly worth a trip to Pondrome to collect them.

'Oh, well,' I said casually, 'if Paul wants them collected I suppose it will have to be done.'

'He wants you to go tomorrow,' Armand said, watching me curiously, 'and bring the stuff back. You will have to go by road and return by train, catching the two o'clock back to Brussels from Pondrome.'

'That means an early start,' I commented.

'Six o'clock,' he nodded, 'in the Place Altitude Cent. You'll carry a

34

picture postcard in your left hand and have your right thumb bandaged. Walk round the Place in an anticlockwise direction. There'll be
a man with a motorcycle. Make sure he sees the bandage and the
postcard.'

'What then?' I asked, scarcely able to repress a smile.

'He will ask you the time, to which you'll answer: "Seven o'clock".
He will say, "Surely you mean eight o'clock." You then get on his bike
and he'll take you as far as Namur.'

'Then?'

Armand went on to tell me how the rest of the journey would be
accomplished. Paul would be waiting for me every hour from 7 to 10
p.m. the next evening at the junction of the Rue de Hetre and the
Avenue Jupiter, for it was impossible to know precisely when the train
would arrive.

'Have you any idea why Paul should want the concrete blocks
collected?' Armand asked, when he had finished briefing me.

'None,' I answered shortly. 'About getting stuff on the black market,
I've got a whole list of things I need.'

Armand took me first to a restaurant in the Place Albert where I
was introduced to the proprietor.

'I shall be delighted to serve Monsieur at any time,' he said, smiling.

'Excellent,' I replied. 'I shall come in quite often.'

He raised his hand as if to say that I should not go away and disappeared into the kitchen. A second later he was back, waving a bottle
in the air.

'I even have this for Monsieur,' he beamed, handing me the bottle.
It was labelled: 'Al Sauce Anglaise'.

Our next destination was a dairy nearby.

'Ah, Monsieur Armand,' cried the woman behind the counter. 'How
are you?'

'Well,' Armand replied. 'We would like a short chat, in private if
that is possible.'

We were led into the sitting-room at the back of the shop.

'My friend,' Armand explained, 'will be needing a lot of things during the next few months. Can you fix him up?'

'Nothing simpler,' the woman replied. 'If Monsieur will give me a list of what he wants, we can have it ready for him in twenty-four hours.'

'As it happens I have a list prepared,' I said, handing her the note which I had written out the previous evening.

'I can let you have a lot of these things right away,' she said, glancing through it.

I was able to leave with some food, cigarettes, tobacco for Monsieur Léon and even some chocolates for his wife. At a stationer's I bought a picture postcard and a large map of Brussels and, at a chemist's, a roll of bandage. After Armand had left me, I went into another stationery shop and bought squared paper, erasers, pencils, a writing pad and a penknife. I was all ready to start work; I lacked only the most essential thing of all – my wireless set.

I went to bed early. The sky was heavy as I drew the blinds, so I was not surprised when I woke the next morning to find that it had rained hard during the night. Already, however, it was clearing up and by the time I left the house at 5.45 there was the promise of a fine day. The city was almost deserted; the first trams swung through the streets with a hollow clatter. The Place Altitude Cent was quite empty except for a young man astride a motorcycle. The ritual, however, had to be observed. I started to walk round the square in an anti-clockwise direction.

As I came abreast of the young man, he said, 'I wonder if you could tell me the time?'

'Certainly,' I said, exposing my postcard and my bandaged thumb. 'It has just struck seven.'

'Surely you mean eight,' he replied, smiling. I smiled too and he said, 'My name is Jean-Claude.' I forget what I said my name was.

Anyone observing this performance would have known – had he ever read a spy book in his life – that we were up to no good, whereas if I had just walked up to the young man and shaken his hand and climbed on to the bike nobody would have suspected a thing. As it was, there was no one about, so our little game was played out in safety.

I swung myself on to the pillion, Jean-Claude let in the clutch and we were on our way, skidding and bouncing over the glistening cobbles. I had intended to arrange some kind of cover story with him, but this was now impossible. I have never been so shaken up. I clung on to the little bar in front of the pillion seat as we jittered and plunged through the still sleeping town. Soon we were flying through the Forêt de Soignes, then through Genval and Ottignies. As we swung into a small village, Jean-Claude pointed out the ruins of a factory which stood beside the road.

'R.A.F. did it a few weeks ago,' he shouted. 'In daylight.' I nodded to show I had heard him and we accelerated sharply. It had certainly been an amazingly accurate piece of bombing for, though the factory was quite destroyed, the rest of the village in which it stood was totally undamaged except for the immediately adjacent houses which had suffered slightly from the blast.

It was 7 o'clock when we pulled up in Namur. The town and our next contact were both asleep. When we had pulled the bell several times, a head and a pair of shoulders appeared at a second-floor window.

'What's all the trouble? Who's there?'

'It's Jean-Claude.' This seemed sufficient and I was glad we did not have to vouchsafe any further information. The door was opened and we were asked in by a man in his pyjamas.

'Aren't you ready?' demanded Jean-Claude.

'Ready? Ready for what?'

'For the next part of this bloke's journey.'

'What journey?' asked our new friend, whose name was René.

'You've had instructions, haven't you?'

René shook his head. 'Not a word.'

'*Merde.*'

'Where's he got to go?'

'Dinant, and quickly.'

'All in good time,' René promised. 'But first we must have some breakfast. Come in.'

At breakfast I suggested that we should arrange some kind of cover story before we started. Both Jean-Claude and René burst out laughing. I flushed; it seemed that they thought one rather nervy to suggest anything of that kind. London-trained agents often found themselves accused of being 'yellow' when they tried to put some security principle into effect. The Belgians' attitude was that they had been doing subversive work for much longer than we had and that their rough-and-ready methods had always proved to be as trustworthy as any we had been able to suggest. Our caution was too like fussiness; they preferred to rely on their wits and their sense of danger to keep them out of trouble. In many cases this was remarkably effective, for they knew exactly how to play upon the unimaginatively methodical mind of the average German. Perhaps the ease with which they outwitted him led them to despise the method which we attempted to impose upon them. One Belgian wireless operator had been caught in a control while actually carrying his set in a small attaché case. He was forced to open it and asked to explain the contents.

'It's an electric massage machine,' he said. 'I'm taking it to be repaired.'

He went on to give such an exhaustive account of the machine and of its supposed defects that the German policeman who was conducting the search waved him on impatiently. Another Belgian had papers which could not stand up to investigation, so he carried a number of obscene photographs in his wallet. These so diverted the Germans that they scarcely looked at his papers. For my part, however, I could never persuade myself to trust quite so blindly in luck; of course, it was impossible to avoid being caught without having a fair share of good fortune, but it seemed unnecessarily foolhardy to rely upon that exclusively.

After breakfast, René took me to collect his motorbike.

'I shouldn't do it,' he said, 'but since I've kept you waiting a bit I'll take a risk and lift you all the way to Pondrome.'

'Are you sure it'll be all right?'

'Hop on,' was his answer.

It was a lovely drive along the banks of the Meuse. There was a control on the bridge at Dinant where we had to cross, but we were not challenged. Since our two stories would probably not have tallied in any particular I was not ungrateful for this let-off. At 11 o'clock René dropped me outside the Café de la Paix at Pondrome. He waved goodbye and charged off along the road we had just travelled.

I watched him go and then turned and went into the café. It was typical of the small village *estaminet*. There was a wooden bar with a single beer tap set in it; four tables with their plain wooden tops scrubbed to ivory whiteness and smoothness filled the tiled bar-room. There were no customers about.

'Monsieur desires?' asked the barman.

'A beer,' I said.

I took my beer to one of the tables and sat down. Then I removed my picture postcard from my inside pocket and placed a pencil on it, according to the detailed instructions which Armand had given me in the Parc Duden. After I had sipped for ten minutes I heard a motorcycle come into the courtyard next to the café. It was not long before its rider came in. He was a man of 55–60 years with a mane of grey hair and deep, intelligent eyes; he looked in the prime of life. Ordering a beer also, he came and sat down at the table next to mine.

'We're in for a fine spell,' he observed.

'It looks like it.'

'Still, autumn is on its way. There's not long to wait now before the leaves fall and Churchill begins his work as liberator.'

Churchill and liberator were the two words which I had been told to listen for, so I knew now that this was without doubt my contact. I picked up my postcard and my pencil and smiled at him to show that I had heard him clearly. He moved his drink to my table.

'I think we ought to have an early lunch here,' he told me. 'We can attend to business later. We've got plenty of time.'

'As you say.'

'My name is Gaston,' he went on. 'I'm the fellow that Guillaume asked to get in touch with the men in the woods.'

'Have you managed to get any more out of them?' I asked.

'Only the concrete blocks,' he replied, 'but Paul seemed particularly keen to have them.'

'Where are they now?'

'They're in my house, in the cellar, together with your case.'

'Where's your house?'

'Near Beauraing.'

We were there by 1 o'clock. Gaston at once took me down to a basement room which was filled with junk. In one corner there was a large pile of potatoes; burrowing through this, he produced my attaché case and three concrete blocks.

'I'd like a hammer and chisel,' I said.

He went into a small room off the basement and came back with the tools which I had asked for. He handed them to me and watched me curiously as I knelt down and began gingerly to chip away the corner of one of the blocks. The coating of concrete was like thin biscuit and it flaked off quite easily, exposing a layer of wire netting. I pulled at this with a pair of pliers and soon the whole of one side of the block was torn away. I was surprised to find that there was no metal box inside, for that was the way my set should have been packed. I held the block up to the light. It was stuffed with bundles of paper and each piece of paper was a 1,000-franc note, worth something over £5. I managed to mask my astonishment from Gaston and, in fact, soon realized what had happened. Because the blocks had been found near my suitcase both Paul and I had assumed that they were the packages containing the wireless, whereas actually they had been Paul's blocks all the time. It was useless to attempt to conceal the contents from Gaston, who was goggling at them with the expression of a man who has just struck gold. I opened the other two blocks and found that they too were packed with currency notes. Suddenly Gaston burst out laughing; it started with a little smile and then, gradually, his whole body began to shake with laughter. I was rather peeved at the way things had turned out (nor did I relish the idea of carrying so much money through the streets of Brussels) and enquired angrily what was so funny.

'That,' he answered thickly, pointing to the stacks of money. 'If they only knew what was in those blocks!' And he was off again.

My attaché case was almost empty (many of the things in it having been stolen) so I was able to pack the notes into it. All the same, I had to sit on the lid before I could get it closed.

'By the way,' Gaston said, 'I've got something else here that may interest you. It was dropped to some local chaps by the R.A.F. and they don't know how to use it.'

I found that the 'thing' was a small radio.

'I know how to use it,' I told him, 'but there's no time to explain now. I must get to Pondrome by two o'clock in case the train is on time.'

'As you wish,' he said.

I picked up my case and we went upstairs, where I stood by the motorbike while Gaston straddled it and tried to start it up. I looked anxiously at my watch. He kicked again and again at the starter pedal, but nothing happened. We checked the petrol and found that there was plenty; we tickled the carburettor and tried again. It was futile. Gaston tried running the bike along the road and leaping on to it. I held the plug terminal while he returned the engine. We pulled the magneto apart and tried to spot the flaw. Two o'clock passed.

'It's no use,' I said irritably. 'We've missed the train. Even if it hasn't actually gone yet I'm not prepared to hang around the station with a case worth a fortune liable to be opened by some nosey Boche.'

Gaston went into the house to look at the local timetable. 'There's a train from Dinant at five,' he reported. 'If you got that you'd be in Brussels between seven and eight.'

'That's all very well,' I said, 'but how in hell am I going to get to Dinant?'

'All we have to do is get the bike repaired and I'll take the risk and run you in.'

'All!' I retorted.

My doubts were justified: the make-and-break-arm spring was broken and, as we were without spares, irreparable.

'That's done it,' Gaston muttered, straightening up.

'Is there any chance of borrowing a car or hiring one?' I asked.

'Not a hope. You can't get permits to drive and I don't know anyone who'd have one.'

'What about borrowing a bicycle?'

'You'd never make Dinant in time. It's over twenty kilometres.'

'Somehow I've got to make it in time,' I said. Gaston kicked morosely at the useless motorbike as I sat down on a bench by the front door of the house.

'I know,' he cried suddenly. 'The ambulance!'

'The what?'

'The local ambulance. The driver's a friend of mine. And he's the sort who'd help us.'

Gaston hurried indoors and I heard him telephoning. In a few minutes he returned.

'He's on his way,' he assured me. 'And he'll take you to Dinant. He's got a permit to run on petrol within a radius of forty kilometres.'

We went indoors to wait for the ambulance. At 3 o'clock a shabby Ford V8 with a wooden body pulled up outside the house. A man in a short white jacket climbed out of the cab and went round to the back of the vehicle. He opened the double doors and drew a stretcher from the interior.

'I'll go and give Raoul a hand,' Gaston told me.

'I'll come too,' I said.

'No,' said Gaston, 'you stay here.'

I was left alone and I heard them talking in the passage, but I could not distinguish what they were saying. At last they came into the room where I was waiting.

'Gaston's explained the situation,' Raoul said curtly. 'I'll take you to Dinant.'

'Thank you,' I replied.

'It's all right,' he went on, 'but you'll have to travel as a casualty. The Boches are suspicious of the ambulance and there's a control where we cross the Meuse. Gaston, we'll need some blood.'

Gaston went out the back way and Raoul turned back to me.

'Give me your coat,' he ordered. 'Take your tie off and open your shirt at the neck.'

I gave him my coat. He went out into the roadway and I looked out of the window to see what he was doing. He bundled the coat into a ball and wiped it in the gutter, turned it inside out and did the same again and then came back into the house.

'What was that in aid of?' I asked angrily.

'You've been knocked down by a car. Near Beauraing. You'd better go and kneel in the gutter now and get your trousers dirty.'

I did as he said.

'You've got a fractured skull,' he told me when I returned, 'so make sure you're unconscious when we're stopped.'

Next he opened a little pot he had with him and rubbed some greenish grease on my face and neck, then took out a bandage. Gaston, having killed a chicken or a rabbit or something, came back with a saucer of blood. Raoul wound the bandage around my head and poured some of the sticky blood into it. Then he went and got the stretcher and a couple of blankets. I lay down on the stretcher and they covered me with the blankets.

'I must have my attaché case,' I groaned.

They hid it under the blankets, between my legs, and we were ready to go. Gaston went outside to make sure that there were no inquisitive onlookers and then they carried me out to the ambulance. So realistic were the preparations that I was beginning to feel quite genuinely ill. They closed the doors of the ambulance, Raoul climbed in and we drove off at high speed. I shall never know how I avoided rolling off the stretcher as the vehicle rocked along the uneven roads. My arms were pinioned by the blankets and I could do nothing to steady myself.

'This is it,' Gaston shouted to me as we approached the bridge. 'Don't move a muscle.'

I felt the ambulance swing to the right and knew that we had turned on to the bridge. We slowed down.

'Halt!'

The ambulance stopped.

'What have you got in there?'

'An accident case,' Raoul said. 'Suspected fracture of the skull.'

'How did it happen?'

'Knocked down by a non-stop car near Beauraing.' Perhaps they would not bother to look. I tried to relax and to control the speed of my breathing. I seemed to be panting.

'Open up,' came the voice of the German.

Footsteps came to the back of the vehicle. The doors were opened and a cold blast of air blew in. My head was at the same end as the door and the temptation to open my eyes was terrifyingly persistent. My eyelids flickered with the effort to keep them closed. My heart pumped. What were they doing? Would it matter if I just blinked? I clenched my fists under the blankets with the strain of not opening my eyes.

The doors slammed shut and we started forward. Soon we turned off the bridge and Raoul shouted back to me, 'What fools they are!'

'Thank God for it,' I replied.

We drove straight into the hospital courtyard. Once there, Raoul jumped out and closed the double gates. He then opened the doors at the back of the ambulance and, with the help of an orderly whom evidently he knew, I was lifted out and carried into a garage where I was unwrapped from my blankets.

'That's that,' Raoul said.

The orderly showed me into a small room where there was a basin. I took off my bandage and washed off the blood and the green make-up. Raoul came in and said to the orderly, 'My friend has got to catch the five o'clock to Brussels. Make sure that he gets on it; it's important.'

'It'll be all right,' the man said.

'I must go now,' said Raoul, holding out his hand. I shook it, and he left. A minute later I heard the ambulance starting up.

The orderly left me in the garage and went to change his clothes. When he returned in civilian dress we left the hospital together and he led me through quiet side streets until we came to a small café. We went through to the back and then down some steps behind a greasy screen, through a rough wooden door and into a cellar. Three men were playing cards, sitting on packing cases round a small polished table. The cellar was grimy and dark, lit by an electric bulb hung from the crumbly plaster of the ceiling. It seemed very lonely; we had seen few people on our way to it.

'Our friend has to get on the five o'clock to Brussels,' the orderly explained. 'It's important.'

I glanced down in a rather nervous way and saw that I was holding my case in front of me; the men seemed to be looking at it. I realized suddenly that I was an outlaw who was carrying thousands of pounds' worth of old notes; if I was knocked out or thrown into the Meuse no one would be any the wiser. I had no identity. Only Paul would miss me and he was scarcely in a position to make trouble with the police.

One of the card players rose from the table and wandered behind me towards the staircase we had just come down. Frightened, I glanced from one to the other of the men; they looked hard and tough and ruthless. It was very strange that Gaston's motorbike should work all right until he knew that I had a fortune with me. And why had he made me stay indoors while he went and talked to Raoul? There was nothing to stop him having phoned these men and told them how much I was worth. Paul would never be able to trace me here; he would most likely think that I had run off with the cash. I swung round, panicky, to see what the man behind me was doing. He was putting the latch across the wooden door at the bottom of the steps.

As it turned out, the men were as trustworthy as they were strong; they were members of a local sabotage group and, as we waited for

5 o'clock to come, they recounted some of their adventures to me. Towards 5 o'clock they sent out a scout (the station was quite near) who would let us know when the train was due; this would avoid having to hang around on the platform. The scout returned at 5.15 with the news that the train was signalled.

'One of us will walk ahead of you,' their leader told me, 'and the other two behind. If there's any trouble, we'll start shooting and you run for it. Get back here or to the hospital.'

In the event, I caught the train without incident. We reached the Gare Leopold at 7.30 and I was able to make the 8 o'clock rendezvous with Paul and tell him about all that had happened. He was very upset when I told him the news: he had relied on my wireless soon being in use. Our organization could only function properly if we were in constant wireless contact with Home Station. As usual, Paul was in a tearing hurry to get to a meeting, so he told me to go home and wait for him to get in touch with me.

I must have been more tired than I realized. My trip in the ambulance and my scare in the cellar had both taken some toll of my nervous energy – at least, that is the only reason I can think of for what happened as I was walking back to the Léons. Of course I had always worn officer's uniform when training in England and, equally naturally, I had got in the habit of returning the salutes of other ranks almost automatically. I was walking along one of the main streets when two German privates approached me. I was thinking of nothing in particular, of home or of my wife perhaps, when they came abreast of me and, giving me a smart 'eyes left', saluted. I had returned their salute before I could stop myself. I glanced behind me and saw that I was being followed by a German captain; it was he who was the object of their salute. I must have scratched my head for the next three blocks in an effort to cover my absent-mindedness!

CHAPTER 5

Security Arrangements

Three days passed without any sign of or message from Paul. I had nothing to do all day. I was restless and anxious. There was nothing I could do except sit in my room until I received instructions.

I passed most of the time lying on the floor sunbathing. The sun poured through the open window all day and I was able to restrain my impatience by acquiring a tan. Nevertheless the delay was both irritating and worrying. On the Monday evening I persuaded Monsieur Léon to let me tune into the B.B.C. News at 9 o'clock.

'Do you speak English?' asked the old man.

'Enough to pick up the gist of what they say,' I replied.

As he took me for a rich and well-educated young man, this did not seem to him to be in any way suspicious, and after carefully closing all the shutters and locking the doors I was allowed to tune in. I forget what the news was: I only recall that it was Alvar Liddell reading it. His impassive voice was strangely calming to my nerves.

I had just finished making my bed on the Wednesday morning and was sitting by my open window, uncertain and depressed, when I heard a car turn into the road. Cars were unusual in Brussels and especially so in our cul-de-sac. It must be coming to one of the houses in our road – and the Germans were the only people who had cars. The car drew up outside our house.

I went to the window facing the road, eased back the lace curtain a few inches, then stood against the wall and glanced down into the street. What I saw set my heart thumping in my throat. A black Citroën was parked by the kerb and from it, as I watched, stepped three German soldiers. The driver opened his door and got out of the car too. A black service revolver in his hand, he followed the three soldiers across the pavement to the front door. The sharp insistent crack of the knocker was followed by urgent jangling on the bell.

I let the lace curtain fall back into place, stilled its swinging and crossed to the door. I crept silently up to the attic at the back of the house. Tense with caution, I pushed the skylight open a few inches and peered out. From there I could see the back garden; beyond the garden was a fence and behind that a waste lot strewn with stones and tufted with rough grass, which gave on to a railway cutting. Beyond the fence, commanding the garden, his eyes on the back of the house, was a German soldier, carrying an automatic rifle. There was no way out; I was boxed.

I went back quickly into my room and shut the door, dreading the click of the latch. The front doorbell jangled again harshly. A heavy foot crashed against the door and a moment later it was opened. Loud, confused voices rose to me from the hall. I glanced feverishly round the room. On the table was my writing case and in my writing case were my microphotographs. There was no time to take them out and burn them. I had to trust their flimsy camouflage. Army boots thundered on the stairs.

I sat by the window; I must remain calm. There was a book on the chair and I picked it up, pretended to read, pretended to myself that I was reading, fastened my eyes on the print. The Germans reached the first-floor landing. They were questioning Madame Lebrun, the postman's wife; I could hear her agitated voice, but I could not make out what she said. I stared at that book and tried to recall my cover story, to make it plausible. The talking continued. I sat there, never turning a page, as the voices talked and talked; first Madame Lebrun, then the impatient Germans, then Madame again. I was conscious of two things: myself and those voices. Nothing else existed. An eternity of voices . . .

Suddenly there were boots on the stair once more. I waited, staring at my book. My hearing seemed to be playing me false, it seemed impossible that what I heard was true. The sound of the boots was diminishing; they were going back down the stairs. Not until the front door slammed did I believe my ears. The Germans had left the house. Car doors opened and shut. I sat still. The engine whirred and caught, the car backed up and turned in the narrow roadway. I heard it drive away down the street. Silence.

I wiped the palms of my hands on my knees and rose to my feet. Downstairs Madame Lebrun and Madame Léon were chattering excitedly. I went quietly into the attic and once again looked out of the skylight. The German soldier had turned his back on the house and was walking briskly away across the waste lot.

A few minutes later I went downstairs to find out what it was all about. Between them the two ladies told me what had happened. Madame Lebrun's son, who was a prisoner-of-war in Germany, had escaped from his camp. The Germans had come to warn her that if he came home she must report the fact at once to the local *Kommandantur*. If she hid him she would be sentenced to death.

For some reason they had not thought it necessary to search the house. Had they done so it might have been very awkward for me. Even now I feared that the place might be watched, and an immediate move seemed imperative. But the boy was recaptured a few days later and the house in the cul-de-sac held no further interest for the Germans.

This episode made me realize how important it was to get my cover story up to date; further, it emphasized the necessity of keeping one's head and not panicking as I had so nearly done in the cellar at Dinant. It was very easy to feel that the only hope was to make a bolt for it, and thus reveal what nobody had ever suspected – that one was engaged in subversive work. An agent I heard about had been having a love affair with some woman and was in bed with her one night when, about 4 in the morning, he heard banging on the door downstairs. Looking out of the window, he saw that the Gestapo were raiding the building (they always made arrests in the early hours) and jumped to the conclusion that they were after him. He flung his clothes on and climbed out on to the roof; he was immediately seen, silhouetted against the skyline, and shot dead. It later transpired that the Gestapo never knew of his existence and had come for someone totally unconnected with him. Seeing him bolt, they had fired on him as a matter of course.

The next morning Paul arrived.

'Terribly sorry not to have got in touch sooner,' he said. 'I've been very busy. The Count's wireless man has got through to London with a message from me. I've asked them for an air drop during the next moon period.'

'Whereabouts?'

'Near St Hubert,' he replied. 'Incidentally, you did say that Gaston had a spare radio?'

'That's right.'

'We'll need it. Get it from him and take it to a place called Hatrival; that's quite close to St Hubert. I've arranged a reception committee. I've put Raymond, one of the forest wardens, in charge of it. He's got about half a dozen men.'

'Excellent,' I commented.

'There's one snag: they don't know how to use it, so you'll have to teach them that and make sure they know the drill for the reception. I've asked London for quite a lot of stuff: a couple of wirelesses, some propaganda, more cash, explosives and photographic gear.'

'Quite a collection!'

'And a dozen Stens and ammunition so that we can be properly equipped for the next receptions we hold.'

'It's a good spot, is it?'

'Couldn't be better. It's pretty clear of woods and that sort of thing and it's completely isolated. Unless something goes wrong we can use it indefinitely.'

'When do you want me there?' I asked.

'It's the twenty-sixth of August today and the next moon period

50

begins on the eighth of September; I'd like you to be in Hatrival between now and then.'

'All right,' I said. 'But I'd like to get my papers straight before I go.'

'Get some passport photos taken,' he ordered, 'and I'll see about it. Look, I must dash off now – got a meeting. Meet me at the Normandie café in the Chausée de Waterloo on Saturday morning at ten.'

I had the photographs taken at a small place near St Gille and collected them before I went to my meeting with Paul on Saturday. He was sitting at a small table on the pavement with a *café au lait* in front of him. We shook hands and I sat down.

'What's the news?' I asked, knowing that Paul never bothered about elaborate security precautions. He believed that if one were quite open one would never be suspected of anything. And, at least as far as he was concerned, the system worked excellently.

'They've agreed to September,' he replied, smiling broadly. 'They'll confirm later, but we've got to be ready well before the eighth. I want you to be ready to start work just as soon as we get your sets; there's a lot of work piling up.'

'We'd best see about recruiting a protection team,' I said.

'Exactly. I've already arranged a meeting for tomorrow with someone I think will be able to help us.'

'When and where?' I enquired.

'Be at the Bois de la Cambre at noon. There's a small bridge near the Avenue Louise. I'll be waiting for you. I can let you know about the trip to Hatrival as soon as I've made the arrangements.'

I left Paul, feeling happier about the progress of affairs. At last it looked as though I should be able to start my real job and regard myself as a useful member of the organization. It was in this mood of renewed confidence that I decided to try my hand at black marketeering. I had been getting my meat from the dairy, but the price was very high and I had heard that there was a café near the Bourse where one could get it at wholesale rates. The carriers took their consignments there and one could often get what passed for bargains. I found the place quite easily and sat down by the door to await events.

'Monsieur?'

'*Café filtre*,' I ordered.

The room was quite crowded but I could see no sign of meat. There were a number of rough characters leaning against the bar with glasses of wine in front of them, and the cheap cigarettes which they smoked filled the atmosphere with their bitter fumes. A fan purred in the roof.

After a while the door swung open and a crowd of scruffy, tired-looking men and women came in. They carried cases and brown paper parcels and packages wrapped in newspaper and a cheer greeted their entrance. People crowded forward. The various wrappings were soon discarded and the table-tops became butchers' slabs as the business of marketing began.

'Terrible journey,' I heard one of the carriers say, 'up at six and travelling all day. The crowds and the heat!'

'Train was so full your feet didn't touch the floor,' agreed another.

The slightly sickly smell of warm meat filled the room. Suddenly the door was flung open with a bang and everyone looked up. An enormously fat woman stood on the threshold, holding herself with an air of a Wagnerian prima donna making her first entrance; her beaming face proclaimed her consciousness of the effect she was making. A cheer greeted this apparition.

'Bravo, Martha!' they cried.

Martha stepped down on to the floor of the café, rolling from side to side. As she came past my table one could see the hoops of sweat beneath her arms and a wave of sourness was brought to one's nostrils. Clearly, she too had had a long and hot journey.

'What have you got for us, Martha?' called someone.

'Ah, just wait and see,' she replied, wagging a forefinger as big as a rolling pin.

'Let's see it!'

She unbuttoned her blouse to the cheers of the onlookers, revealing her great breasts.

'It's the meat we want to see, Martha.'

She roared with laughter and, suddenly, put her hand down into her bosom and brought out a huge slab of steak.

'What a magician!' called the barman.

The room rocked with the applause.

'What other tricks do you know?'

'I'll show you,' she cried and plunged her hand once more between her bulbous breasts. Another huge slab of steak was produced and the room went wild. I pushed my way blindly out of the café. I thought I might become a vegetarian.

This café was only one of innumerable clearing houses for small black market dealers. Most of the carriers were poorish people who were lucky enough to have relatives in the country from whom they could buy what food they wanted. They could sell any surplus to restaurants at a price which would give them their own share free and still, most probably, leave a certain profit. In general the black market was not run by large combines, as it was in America during Prohibition, but by small traders and opportunists. The result of this situation was that while the peasant class and their poor town relations were able to subsist quite comfortably and the rich could buy from them what they did not want, the wretched people on small fixed incomes (pensions and annuities) were reduced almost to starvation. Before my arrival the Léons had been in this position and, as my first meal with them proved, had to live almost entirely on unsweetened ersatz coffee and rationed bread. The Germans closed their eyes to the black market since they were likely to find their favourite restaurants unable to serve them if they became too strict. Even if they were caught and fined, these restaurants made such vast profits that their business was unaffected and their habits unchanged.

Uncertain how far it was to the spot where I was supposed to meet Paul on Sunday morning, I set out early. It was always my habit to walk to our various meeting places since this was the only way I could gauge accurately how long it would take me to reach them on another occasion. To travel by tram was to lay oneself open to being held up by controls, which meant waiting while everyone in the tram showed their papers. Controls on the pavement seldom took so long and were, in any case, the easier to avoid.

I entered the park Paul had mentioned at 9.40 and soon found the bridge he had spoken about. It was where the road which ran through the park crossed a small dip; a narrow path thread a way under the bridge and connected the two sides of the park.

I followed it on its course, considering how to pass the time until Paul's arrival. It was early on Sunday morning and there were few people about; an elderly lady exercised a trim poodle up by the park gates and a young couple sauntered along. A snatch of their laughter came to me as I pushed my way through the thick undergrowth which obstructed the path, and I felt lonelier for their presence. Suddenly there was a rustling in the bushes just behind me. Indiscreetly perhaps, I went to see what it was that I had disturbed. I parted the bushes just as someone did the same thing from the other side: it was a young German soldier.

'Excuse me,' I muttered, thinking I had stumbled upon him at a singularly inappropriate time. I stepped back hastily.

There was a muffled grunt as I did so, and I turned to find that another German soldier was lying just beside the path. He was covered in some kind of green netting and now, as I looked around, I saw that the whole area was swarming with Germans disguised as all kinds of natural objects. I gathered from their youth that they were all cadets; clearly I had walked into the middle of their camouflage exercise. I withdrew with all speed and regained the main road just in time to see Paul and a tall young man approaching. I hurried up to them and shook their hands as though I had just met them by chance.

'How lucky it is to bump into you!' I cried.

'Don't be silly,' Paul said, 'you knew we were coming.' (Sometimes Paul's disregard for security became quite militant.)

'Quite,' I replied, smiling, 'but I didn't know the Germans were having a meeting at the same spot.'

'What do you mean?'

I explained, and Paul and his companion appreciated the point of my greeting. We found a more satisfactory part of the park in which to continue our discussion.

'I want you to meet Michel,' Paul said to me when we had sat down. Then, to Michel, 'This is René.'

Michel and I shook hands again. He was a good-looking man of 26 or so, well-built and confident in his bearing. One felt one could trust him.

We got down to business at once. Paul told Michel what we wanted him to do.

'You'll need about four men to carry the set and to act as a protection team when René is actually on the air.'

'I can manage that,' Michel said.

'You'll also need a list of houses you can send from. René will tell you what's wanted.'

I explained how the set should be carried, and the drill which the team should carry out when I was on the air. I also gave him details of the kind of house which was most suitable for the work and the voltage and type of current which I would require.

'I can look after that angle too,' he told us. 'I know a good many people who will be ready to help us.'

'Excellent,' commented Paul. 'It may be a couple of weeks before René is ready to transmit, but you can go ahead with the preparations right away.'

Michel nodded. 'How can we get in touch with each other?' he asked.

'We'd better not know each other's addresses in case anything goes wrong,' Paul said. 'We can arrange for outdoor meetings. They're always safer. I'll act as go-between.'

Two days later Madame Léon stopped me on the way up to my room. 'Monsieur Felix, a man came and told me to tell you that the butter you were expecting has arrived. He didn't say what his name was.'

I thanked Madame and went on upstairs. The message was a

prearranged signal between Paul and myself: I was to meet him at Ma Compagne (a café) at 2.30. Paul was waiting when I arrived. He had a new identity card for me; in it was pasted one of the photographs I had had taken, and it lacked only my signature. I was now Monsieur Henri de Nys. My age was 35, married, and I was employed by the Belgian Railways as a lorry driver, a reserved occupation. Paul also handed me a *carte de travail* and a numbered armband which I was supposed to wear when I was on duty. As opposed to the Monsieur Fournier which I had been until now (according to the papers I had been issued in England), Monsieur de Nys was a real person and I had taken his identity, although he did not know it. This meant that my papers could, to some extent, bear being checked: Monsieur de Nys was a genuine lorry driver and his name was on the books of the railways. On the other hand, were I to be confronted with his wife or taken to the address given on my card, my imposture would be instantly exposed. Still, at least I was somewhat safer.

'We're going to Hatrival tomorrow,' Paul told me. 'But we'll go to Beauraing first and collect the wireless. Meet me at a quarter to six tomorrow morning at the Gare Leopold.'

When I left the Léons at 5.15 the next morning, the streets were dark and deserted. The trams had just started running, however, and I decided, contrary to my usual principle, to take one to the station. I met Paul in the yard, wheeling two bicycles.

'We'll take these in the train,' he said, 'and carry the wireless on them to Hatrival.'

'Right,' I said.

'I'll stay here with the bikes. You go and get a couple of singles to Beauraing and two cycle tickets.'

I went into the station and knocked on the booking-office counter. The clerk shuffled over.

'Two to Beauraing, please, and two cycle tickets.'

'Sorry,' the clerk said, 'no bicycles on the six o'clock.'

'Why?'

'There's no luggage van, that's why. No luggage van, no bicycles.'

I hurried back to Paul and told him what had happened.

'*Merde!* We'll have to change the plan.'

'What's the best thing to do?' I asked, glancing nervously at my watch.

'You press on to Beauraing alone,' he said, 'and get the wireless from Gaston. Take the train from there to Le Poix St Hubert, that's the nearest we can get to Hatrival. I'll meet you there and give you a hand the rest of the way. Clear?'

I nodded and ran back to the booking office. I just caught the train as it began to move out of the station. We arrived in Beauraing just after 10 o'clock. Before setting out to meet Gaston I asked about trains to St Hubert. There was a suitable one just after noon which took five hours. I would have to make two changes, but it was the best I could do.

I found Gaston's house and he was awaiting me.

'I've taken the wireless to a friend of mine,' he told me. 'He lives near the station, so you won't have to lug the thing through the streets. You can pick it up just before your train goes.'

We had an early lunch and then went to Gaston's friend's house. The set was in the cellar, in a small black box.

'Handy little thing,' I remarked.

'You should have seen it when it was dropped. See all those scratches on this side?'

'What about them?'

'It had "THIS SIDE UP" written there in English before I scrubbed it off!'

'Perhaps you could say it was a lifebelt,' Gaston suggested.

'Why should I be carrying a lifebelt on a local train from Beauraing to St Hubert?' I enquired.

'What about a deaf-aid?'

The silence which greeted this suggestion avoided the necessity of rejecting any others, but scarcely made me any the more confident. My train was due, so I carried the black box over to the station and booked my ticket. I went on to the platform and looked for somewhere inconspicuous to put the box. My plan was to leave it somewhere a fair distance away from me so that, in the event of a snap control, I could walk away from it and, if pressed, disclaim all knowledge of it. There was a luggage trolley piled with cases and trunks just near the barrier, so I put my black box just behind it and strolled off down the platform. I reached the end of the covered area and turned back again, just in time to see a porter wheel away the trolley of luggage. My black box was now the only object on the platform.

Shortly after, a German sergeant arrived. He had either been badly wounded or involved in a serious accident, for he walked with great difficulty and the help of two sticks. He stood alone, waiting for the train which at length appeared. I retrieved my black box and climbed aboard. The train was almost full (certainly there were no seats) so I found myself a space in the corridor, parked the box in a dark corner and again moved slightly away from it. The train pulled slowly out of the station. As it began to move, the German sergeant came through the connecting door from the next carriage, dragging himself along by the handrail. He was looking into all the compartments for a seat, but of course there was none, nor did anyone offer him one. Realizing the futility of his search, he propped himself up near me, leaning his back against the door of a compartment.

He smiled hesitantly, then he gave a little cough and said, 'Excuse me, I wonder if you could tell me whether this train with the one for Poix St Hubert connects?'

My first impulse was to shrug my shoulders – the usual gesture of a patriotic Belgian if asked a question by a German – but then I realized that if he were going all the way to Poix St Hubert he would be the ideal companion for a man carrying a wireless set. Besides, he did not seem a bad old chap.

'What excellent French you speak!' I said. He smiled broadly at this unexpected compliment. 'Yes, you're on the right train. I'm going to Poix St Hubert myself.'

Soon we were chatting with the greatest freedom. My fellow-passengers were not pleased with my conduct; whenever they had occasion to pass along the corridor – and this was very frequently – they always contrived to bump me very hard.

'Wounded?' I asked the German.

'That's right. Russian front. In both legs I was shot.'

I shook my head sympathetically. 'How long ago was that?'

'In hospital I have been for several months. I am to a convalescent home going now, near St Hubert.'

'Do the legs still hurt?'

'I cannot stand for long without hurt,' he replied.

'Do you see that black box behind you?' I asked.

'Yes,' he said, glancing towards it.

'It belongs to me,' I said. 'Why don't you sit on it and rest your legs?'

A look of such astonishment passed across his face that I feared he suspected something. I was soon reassured.

'May I really do this?' he asked. 'But you are too kind. I think you are the nicest Belgian that I ever meet. Yes, you *are* the kindest.'

I shrugged and smiled, as if to suggest that I did as much for any German I saw in difficulties. The sergeant sat down on the black box with a grunt of satisfaction.

'Some people have no shame,' I heard someone say from the compartment by which I was standing. Similar comments were made during the rest of the journey, and I was quite bruised by the elaborate bumpings which I received from the relays of people who went along to the lavatory.

When we changed trains, I helped the old fellow (he was about 50 years old, I suppose, with greying hair and a considerable paunch) with his packages. There were plenty of seats on the train into which we changed. The sergeant and I got into an almost empty compartment and I hid my box under his greatcoat and hoped for the best.

We reached Poix St Hubert at 8.30. The sergeant and I climbed out of the train and I said, 'I go this way,' pointing in the opposite direction to the one in which he was heading.

'Oh, what a shame this is,' he replied. 'I am sorry to see you go. I think you are the most charming Belgian I ever meet. I wish there were more like you.' He shook my hand fervently.

'Goodbye,' I said, 'and good luck with the recovery.'

'Thank you, thank you so much.'

He shouldered his kitbag and stumbled off down the road. Paul came out of the little shelter where he had been sitting and shook my hand.

'What's going on?' he asked. 'The Boche seems to have fallen for you.'

I explained what had happened and Paul laughed delightedly. 'The best escort you could have,' he said.

Paul had his bicycle with him, so we strapped the box on to the carrier and walked together to Hatrival. Curfew time in the country was 10 o'clock and as we approached Hatrival we saw that it was just on that hour. Raymond, the forest warden in whose house we were to stay, lived at the far end of the village, so we made a detour and soon found ourselves at the back door of his cottage. Paul gave the prearranged knock and Raymond himself opened the door. He was a tall, well-built man, not unlike Guillaume, the farmer at La Ferme Physic. He led us into a bright kitchen with the table laid for supper. We were introduced to his wife who soon served us with a meal.

We were having coffee when there was a knock at the door and Raymond admitted three men; they were singularly unalike in appearance, for one of them was an elderly man with a thin, intelligent face and a small grey beard, the second was brawny with eyebrows that met across a bull face, while the third was a very pink, rather chubby young man whom one expected to have a lisp.

Paul stood up and shook them all by the hand. I was introduced as René. I unpacked the wireless and spent the next hour trying to instruct my three new friends in its use. I demonstrated how to connect the set, how to tune it and how to charge the accumulators with the trickle charger. I also showed them how it could be used as a rough direction-finder.

This was clear enough and they readily understood what I was telling them; the difficulty came when we got on to the subject of procedure. My pupils professed to know English, but their pronunciation was so bad that, making allowances for the normal distortion of the instrument, I was convinced that they would be unable to make any satisfactory contact between the ground and the aircraft which was doing the drop. I stopped telling them about the wireless and tried to teach them some English. But the accent is the most difficult thing for a continental to learn; certainly it was beyond my ability to teach it in one evening. In the end, in a mood of some exasperation, we sent our three ill-assorted pupils home and decided that either Paul or I would deal with the first reception. Before the second the others would have to practise their English.

After they left Paul said, 'I've got to go back to Brussels first thing tomorrow morning. I've a lot of things to attend to, and I want to hear as soon as possible when the final O.K. for the drop comes through from London. The trouble is that I've got such a hell of a lot to do that I don't think I can possibly get back here for three days at least.'

'I'll tell you what,' I said. 'I'll come back to Brussels by a later train tomorrow and then as soon as you hear from London you can let me know and give me the details. Then I can come straight back here and get on with it.'

'Good idea,' he said. 'That's how we'll work it.'

We went upstairs to bed.

CHAPTER 6

News from the B.B.C.

Paul had left when I awoke the next morning. After breakfast I walked the three miles to the station and found there was a train which would arrive in Brussels around 4 o'clock. I boarded it easily enough and we made good time as far as Namur. There we stopped and waited and waited.

'All change,' came the inevitable call. 'This train is going no further. All change.'

The platform was already crowded with the passengers from a previous train to whom the same thing had happened. An hour later, the 'express' from Nancy steamed in. People grabbed at the handrails as it came slowly to a halt and swung themselves aboard; it was filled before it had stopped. Those who could not get in through the doors wriggled through the wide windows of the compartments into the laps of those already occupying them. Eventually, by what means I know not, everybody who had been on the platform squeezed themselves on to the train. I was forced into a tiny lavatory at the end of one of the coaches. So were thirteen other people. I never moved an inch for an hour and a half; when we steamed into the Gare Leopold it took us nearly a quarter of an hour to extricate ourselves from the lavatory we were packed in it so tightly.

The Léons were not expecting me – I had told them I would be away for a few days – so I went to the restaurant in the Place Albert and had a good meal. I reached home about 9 o'clock feeling very tired, and had just set my foot on the stair when there was a call from the kitchen.

'Is that Monsieur Felix?'

'Yes,' I said warily.

'Would you come for a moment?'

I went along the passage to the kitchen.

'Well?'

'I'm sorry to disturb you, but a young man called with a message for you. He said you were to catch a six-thirty train tomorrow morning and go back to where you've come from.'

'That's fine,' I said.

'Oh, and would you be at the station well before time because your friend wants to see you there before you leave?'

'Thank you so much for giving me the message,' I said sourly. 'I expect I shall be away for several days.'

I woke just after 4.30, dressed in the dark and sneaked out of the house in time to catch the first tram to the station. As we moved away from the stop a squad of about thirty German military policemen suddenly appeared on bicycles and sealed off the road behind us. Ours was the last vehicle they let through.

Paul was waiting at the station entrance; in the gloomy light of early morning he seemed strangely sinister.

'Sorry about this,' he smiled, 'but confirmation's come through. They're definitely making the drop this period. It may come any night of the next ten, tonight included.'

'What's the signal?'

'The B.B.C. will send it over during the personal messages in the French Service between seven-fifteen and seven-thirty at night.'

'Well, what is it?'

'*Mona est une belle blonde.* When you hear that, you'll know delivery is going to be made the same evening.'

'What time?'

'During the first half of the period, between nine-thirty p.m. and one-thirty in the morning; during the second, between eleven-thirty and three-thirty.'

'I see. What's the drop consist of?'

'Five containers and a "body".'

'Body' was our slang for an agent. This particular one was a wireless operator whom we had to deliver to a certain contact in Brussels.

'Right,' I said, 'I'd better be off.'

'This operation is very important for us, Jacques,' Paul said seriously. 'It must be a success; we need those wirelesses and we need a confident team at Hatrival.'

I booked a second-class ticket. It was still dark and the blackout was strict. A blue light which seemed less a light than a reflection of one was the only illumination on the platform. I peered at the sides of the coaches and presently found one marked with a 2; to my surprise there was no one pushing to get into it. I opened the door of the carriage and climbed inside. There were plenty of empty places, so I sat down in a corner seat and made myself comfortable.

A neatly dressed elderly man opposite gave me a curt nod and a slight smile. I smiled and nodded back. A high-ranking German officer passed along the coach; he was followed by several well-dressed civilians. Outside, on the platform, people rushed about looking for places in the train. Except for the coach I was in, it seemed to be packed. I leaned forward towards my elderly fellow-passenger and, as he did the same towards me, I asked politely:

'This is the right part of the train for Poix St Hubert, isn't it? Or is it reserved or something?'

The little man at once went purple in the face and started shouting in a very tempestuous manner. The other people in the carriage did the same. Too indignant to speak French, they pointed fiercely to a notice painted in whitewash on the windows. It read: WEHRMACHT ONLY. I grabbed my suitcase and scrambled out of the compartment. It was the first and last time I was ever taken for a member of the Gestapo.

Raymond and his wife were delighted with the news I was able to give them. I spent all afternoon checking the wireless and assuring myself that it was in working order. Raymond's wife was making some coffee when the telephone rang; the call was for me.

'Is that you, Jacques?' a voice asked. I recognized it at once; it was Paul.

'Yes,' I said. 'What is it? Is something wrong?'

'Not exactly,' he answered. 'It's just that Mona's been held up and can't be along for four days or so.'

This was a disappointment, of course, but it did give us time to make our preparations more thorough. The main section of our reception team was living in a hut in the woods; there were six of them there, all *réfractaires* who were actively engaged in resistance work. They could be contacted from Hatrival in about half an hour, while of the other members of our team two had wirelesses and could listen for the message themselves and get in touch with those who were unable to do so. The hut in the woods was between us and the dropping ground so, on the critical evening, we could pick up our colleagues on our way there.

I suggested that it would be a good idea if, the next day, I briefed the men in the hut about their duties when it came to the reception of the drop.

'We'll go and see them,' Raymond said. 'The only thing is that I'm a little worried about a stranger being seen around the village. You don't look much like a countryman.'

'Raymond,' his wife said, 'surely you could put him in your spare uniform?'

'Excellent idea!' Raymond agreed. 'Then you can spend your time with me and we can get through the woods without anyone asking awkward questions.'

Raymond was over six feet, whereas I am five feet seven or so. Nevertheless, with the help of a stitch of two to keep the cuffs turned back, and an extra hole in the belt, I was able to look fairly present-able. I put on the hat Raymond gave me; it had its brim turned up at the back and down at the front and a lanyard round the crown from which two little acorns dangled. I was to be Raymond's assistant in marking trees for felling.

The next morning the weather was fine and Raymond and I set off soon after breakfast; he was carrying a knapsack with our lunch in it, as we would not be back before dusk. The country had a very pleasant effect upon me; I felt relaxed and happy – not shut in, as one did sometimes in Brussels. We passed a number of people working in the fields and they waved to Raymond as we went; no one seemed interested in me.

The countryside was mainly covered by plantations of pine trees, some privately and some publicly owned; there were also tracts of natural forest where the wild boar could still be hunted. One could travel through these forests only by following the official paths which ran through them; on either side, the tangled and impenetrable undergrowth forbade entrance. We followed the path for some distance and then Raymond branched off down a gap in the brush, through the trees.

'Don't break the undergrowth,' he said, turning back to me, 'push it aside so it bars the way again. We mustn't make a path here whatever we do.'

Raymond led me on a zigzag route which I did my best to follow exactly. He stepped high over ferns and always managed to find a bare surface on which to put his feet so that there were no trails of bruised grass left behind us. We ducked under low branches and dodged saplings; all the while I concentrated on playing an exact game of follow-my-leader. Raymond stopped and gave a special whistle. There was no reply the first time, but when he stopped again and repeated it there came an answering call. A moment later we had emerged into a small clearing where the hut had been built.

I had already met two of the six men who lived there, and now I was introduced (again as René) to the others. The hut was very firmly built (thanks, mainly, to Raymond) out of small pine trunks plugged with bracken; the roof was roughly thatched. They had no natural water there; the nearest water was half a mile away, which meant that each day someone had to wheel a bicycle through the woods with two ten-gallon milk churns strapped to it and still leave as little trace as we had done.

'What do you do all day?' I asked.

They laughed. 'That's the trouble,' said one. 'There isn't a thing to do.'

'Except sabotage; we do a bit of that.'

'What sort of thing?' I asked.

'We blew up a small transformer station a few miles from here and then we fixed the oil store at St Hubert—'

'How did you get the explosive for blowing the thing up?' I asked.

'We'll show you where we got that,' they smiled, 'when we've finished the briefing.'

The arrangements for receiving the drop were explained in general terms, then I gave them the details of their particular tasks: who I would require to carry the signal torches which would tell the aircraft the line to take at the run-in; who I wanted as my runner; which of them should carry guns and deal with any intruders who might arrive; which should act as look-outs for the actual drop. Of course, these postings took into account not only the men in the hut but also those from the village who were to help us.

When I had gone over all the details again to make sure that nothing had been missed, one of the men said he would take us, if we liked, to see where they got their explosives. He led us a long way into the woods and stopped in a clearing at the bottom of a shallow valley.

'Well, can you see anything?' he asked, grinning.

I shook my head. Our guide walked over to a patch of bracken and held it apart, revealing a large metal cylinder which appeared to be embedded in the soft earth. It was a 1,000lb bomb. I suppose it had been jettisoned by one of our planes and had failed to go off. Apparently the case was cracked when they found it; with amazing daring, the men in the hut had broken away the base of the bomb, levering the crack open wider, and were now able to scoop out the explosive. They covered it with a waterproof to protect it from the rain.

Raymond and I went on to take a look at the reception ground and found it ideal; there was even a small haystack – brown, matted and abandoned – from the top of which I should be able to use the wireless. This would greatly increase my range and so make the task of preparation easier. Apart from a rough stone track which straggled across it, the field was covered with soft grass, ideal for the 'body'. The field was quite isolated, the nearest farm being over a mile away.

Once we had checked the dropping ground and briefed our team there was nothing left to do but wait. I went out with Raymond when he was on his job; the new 'forester' was now taken for granted. Every evening we tuned in to the B.B.C. at 7.15 to hear the personal messages; there was just a chance that ours might be included. The jamming was very bad and we had to turn the volume up full to hear the voice behind the squawk of the interference. We covered the window with two blankets so that the noise could not be heard outside. The voice swelled and faded through the jamming.

'*Le chat n'aime pas le chien . . . Message pour Jean – non . . . Le lièvre est dans les betraves . . . Cinq et sept sont douze . . . Message pour Yves – oui, je repéte – oui . . . Marie et Helene embrassent Madeleine et Jean.*'

Our message did not come. The weather was fine, but on the fourth day the wind freshened; if it increased to over 20 miles an hour it would be dangerous to accept the 'body'. But when would the 'body' come? Somewhere in England a Halifax was waiting to carry him to us; somewhere he himself was watching to see if his name was on the ops board. We returned at the end of this fourth day to find Paul waiting for us. When he saw me he burst out laughing; I could not understand what was so funny until I realized that it was the first time he had seen me in my forester's uniform.

We waited for 7.15, for this was the first evening when we could reasonably expect to hear Mona's name from London. I checked that the wireless was in working order. We were very keyed-up.

Seven o'clock. We turned on the radio. Paul lit a cigarette. So did I. Smoke swirled under the light bulb. Nobody spoke.

'*Veuillez écouter, s'il vous plait, à quelques messages personelles.*' The impersonal voice of the announcer came through the whine of the jamming. '*Le chat n'aime pas le chien . . . le lièvre est dans les betraves . . . le bateau arrive . . . la lune est claire . . . sept et neuf sont des numéraux impairs . . . le pluie tombe . . .*' I looked at my watch. Five minutes had gone. '*Message pour André – nous disons oui . . . Pierre, Jean vous attend ce soir si la mer est calme . . . les oiseaux sont bleus . . .*' Ten minutes were gone. '*Le vent est froid; nous répétons – le vent est froid . . . Mona est une belle blonde . . . Message pour Jean-Paul . . .*' It took a minute to realize that we had really heard the words, then we all jumped up and started to talk at once.

'Hope the others heard it.'

'Let's get going.'

'This is it.'

We put on our coats, gloves and scarves (the evenings were cold); I had my wireless under my overcoat which I buttoned up over it.

We left by the back door and Raymond led the way across the dark allotments behind the cottage. No one said anything until we were clear of the village. The night was clear and cold; the shadows cast by the moon were like knives across the path. There was frost on the ground.

'How much stuff do you think they'll drop us?' I asked, when we had reached the cover of the woods.

'I don't know,' Paul replied. 'I've asked for a hell of a lot, but I don't suppose they'll send it all. Anyway, we know Ping-Pong's coming and they'll drop a few containers as well.'

'Ping-Pong?'

'That's our "body's" code name.'

The men in the hut greeted us enthusiastically. It was now nearly 8 o'clock and the plane would not arrive for at least another hour and a half, so we settled down to some hot coffee and discussed last-minute plans.

'We ought to leave someone here,' one of the men said, 'in case anyone comes snooping round.'

'We need everyone we've got,' I put in.

'Don't worry,' Paul said. 'If we get half the stuff I've asked for, we shall be able to give any unwelcome visitors something to remember.'

Paul's comment reassured our friends and we all left the hut shortly afterwards. Paul and one of the local men went ahead to meet the other four members of our team (those who lived in the village) and contacted them without difficulty; in a few minutes we were entering the large field which Raymond and I had visited a few days earlier.

Our guards were issued with automatics and sent to patrol the perimeter of the field. The others knew their various jobs when the time came and now disposed themselves in the best positions to carry them out. My runner was with me; the torch-bearers were posted ready to light up; Paul was at the assembly point; the spotters were already straining their eyes for the dropping parachutes. I climbed up on to my haystack. The vigil began.

Every few minutes I would switch on my radio and speak slowly, clearly into the microphone: 'H for Halifax calling S for Sugar. H for Halifax calling S for Sugar. Can you hear me? Can you hear me? I cannot hear you. I cannot hear you.'

There was no reply, so I switched off and removed my headphones. It was now very cold and, as if the world were contracted by the coldness itself, distant sounds were sharp and clear; the whistle of a train (bitten off by a tunnel and then keening forth again as the train emerged), the yapping of a farm dog, the rustle of leaves.

Below the haystack men whispered in the darkness. Two hours passed. Paul came round with a flask of brandy and we all had a good pull at it. I heard more whispering below me as Paul joined the group under the haystack; they seemed to be asking him something and in a few seconds I learned what it was. There came the rasp of a match being struck and soon cigarettes glowed at the corners of the field.

Three hours passed, then I heard quite distinctly the hum of an aircraft. I started sending out my message in the direction he was pointing, following the plane across the sky. No reply came through. Soon the aircraft had disappeared.

News from the B.B.C.

Half an hour later I was again sending out my message when Paul came round with the last ration of brandy.

'How are you, old boy?' Paul called.

'Cold,' I said.

'I'll take over shortly and you can try and warm up a bit.' Once more I started trying to get into communication with the plane. Suddenly I heard the answer loud and clear.

'They're here!' I cried. 'They're here. I can hear them.'

'Tell them, not us,' Paul shouted.

'Have I the pleasure of addressing Mr H for Halifax?' asked the calm voice of the plane's captain.

'Indeed you have,' I cried. 'Am I glad to hear you, S for Sugar! I thought you were never coming.'

'Sorry we're a bit late, old chap. I say, can you hear our engines at all?'

I pushed back my earphones and called to the men below, 'Can you hear anything?'

'Not a sound,' was the answer.

I heard Paul shouting orders away on the far side of the field.

'Not a thing,' I said into the microphone. 'Send me a tuning count and I'll try and give you a rough bearing.'

'One, two, three, four, five, six, seven, eight, nine, ten . . .' I swung round as the voice came through and found that it faded as I faced north. 'One, two, three, four . . .'

'I say,' I cut in, 'you're flying south of us.'

'Did you say south, repeat south?'

'Affirmative.'

I could hear him giving instructions to his crew over the intercom. One of the men nearby signalled to me and pointed to the south-west. I removed my earphones: in the distance I could hear the hum of an approaching plane.

'Runner,' I called. 'Get hold of Paul and tell him to send out the morse letter.'

My runner disappeared into the gloom. The aircraft's engines swelled into a roar, but we could not see it. Suddenly two long flashes appeared out of the sky – the morse letter M.

'Red lights on!' Paul shouted.

The plane was almost overhead.

'I can see your lights quite well,' called the captain. 'I'll circle round to get into position. Tell your boys to follow me round with their lights.'

My runner took these orders to Paul. The plane started to sweep round. As it did so I gave the pilot the wind direction and speed: 'Wind north, five m.p.h.'

'North, five per hour.'

'Affirmative. What are you bringing us?'

'One "body" – two packages – four containers – four pigeons.' I repeated this to Paul who translated it into French for the benefit of the team. Meanwhile, the plane circled wide and the sound of its engines died away.

Some of the men holding the lights thought it was going away and either put them out or forgot to point them in the direction of the aircraft.

'I say, old chap, your lights have disappeared. You're not in trouble, are you?'

Paul hurried off to check what was up and soon the four lights were again visible to the plane. The pilot was too far to starboard now and had to make another full circle.

'Will you drop the "body" and one package first?' I asked, as this manoeuvre was completed. 'Then three containers, and the other container, the second package and the pigeons last.'

'Right you are. Just keep off the air now, old chap, and I'll give the crew the gen.'

The plane approached the field on its run, coming in at about 600 feet, engines throttled down.

'Action stations!' I heard over the intercom. The "body" was sitting, I could imagine, as I had done, legs dangling, arms braced. 'GO!'

We were all staring upwards as we saw something drop from the belly of the plane; in a second the parachute puffed open. A second followed it.

'Chutes safely away,' I called to the captain.

The plane banked away. The two camouflaged parachutes reached the ground, so far as I could see well inside the field.

'"Body" and package safely landed,' my runner reported.

I passed the message on to the aircraft.

'Good show, boys, good show!' was the reply.

'Had a good journey tonight?' I asked.

'Can't complain, old chap. Bit of flak, you know, as we crossed the coast, but not much of a show. I say, you speak the lingo pretty well. Britisher by any chance?'

'Certainly am. Wish we could have a drink together.'

'Drink? Think I could land my kite in your field for a quick one?'

The plane was running in again. As it passed overhead three more chutes dropped from it, and our men dashed off to try to spot where they landed. The plane circled away again and then turned in for its final run. The last package and the last container were dropped and then something quite small fell out from the aircraft; there seemed to be no parachute attached to it and it fell heavily some sixty yards from me. My runner went to see what it was; he brought back the wreckage of a small chute and the corpse of a pigeon.

'What went wrong with the pigeon?' I enquired of the pilot.

'Must have hit the plane on the way down.'

'That's right,' another voice interrupted. 'Something hit one of the elevators after the other two chutes were away.'

It was clear that the boxes which held the pigeons were too light and so were snatched by the slipstream and shattered against the fuselage. Further deliveries were always made with weighted boxes.

The aircraft turned for home.

'Good luck on the way home,' I called.

'All the best yourself.'

I switched off the wireless, jumped down off the haystack and went to the assembly point. Paul was there with Ping-Pong.

'How was the landing?' I asked.

'Nice and soft, thanks. No trouble at all.'

'Nothing's to be unpacked,' Paul said sharply as the men brought in the canisters, 'until we're sure it's all here.'

All the containers were accounted for, but we had only one of the pigeons (the dead one my runner had found) out of the four which had been dropped. It was fairly certain that they were all dead and so might be found by anyone who visited the field. If they knew anything about pigeons they would be sure to recognize them as carriers. It could not be helped, however, so we set about unpacking. One of the packages was Ping-Pong's, the other was addressed to me (under my code name 'Hillcat'). It contained two wireless sets; there was also a large sealed envelope marked 'HILLCAT – PERSONAL', which I put in my pocket.

We called in the guards from the perimeter. Paul divided the load among the assembled team and, Raymond leading, we set off back through the woods. The load was very heavy and we were fagged out when we reached the hut. We dumped the stuff outside and went in. The kettle was put on the stove. When the coffee was made, we brought in the packages and unpacked them. Apart from propaganda material, money and films, we had a consignment of cigarettes, tobacco, chocolate, bully beef and, to the unrestrained pleasure of the company, a flask of whisky. We toasted our success and the homeward journey of S for Sugar. This was, I later discovered, safely accomplished.

Soon it was time to go. Paul, Raymond, Ping-Pong and I gathered up our part of the load and made our way back to Hatrival. It was just after 4 in the morning when we arrived there. Paul had brought a large empty suitcase with him in which we packed the films and the propaganda. Paul and Ping-Pong would take the three sets and Ping-Pong's personal suitcase with them; I would follow with Paul's.

The others left early the next morning, but I did not wake till midday. Raymond came with me to the station, wheeling my heavy suitcase on his bicycle. The case contained hundreds of mimeographed copies of *The Times*, propaganda stickers (to go over German posters), a copy of *Desert Victory* and hundreds of calendars for 1944 (on each of which Hitler was portrayed wiping his bottom).

I reached Brussels at 6.30 that evening. The train had been so crowded that there was no possibility of a control, but now I was on my own, staggering down the Grand Boulevard, and the situation was unpleasingly different. The case weighed a ton. I shifted it from one hand to the other, walked a few yards, then slung the case ill-temperedly back to the other hand. As I did so the handle, frayed no less than my temper, snapped and the case fell to the ground with the thudding finality of a knocked-out heavyweight. I lifted it and clutched it to my bosom, but had managed only a few yards more when I heard a tearing sound. The leather hinge which supposedly strengthened the back was splitting slowly from end to end, and a calendar (Hitler's bottom) began to push through the gap. Tottering, I carried the case to a bench and deposited it there. The split was nearly a foot long and already the stitching farther along was danger-ously extended. I would have to rope it up somehow. But my rain-coat had no belt; my sock suspenders were too short; my braces were indispensable. Only my tie remained. It just went round and after numerous attempts I was able to tie some kind of a knot to secure it. I sat down beside the damned case and rested.

I had to deliver the case to Paul at 9 o'clock, so there was no point in going all the way home. I decided to go to the restaurant in the Place Albert; it was on the way to our meeting place. I lifted my case and lumbered towards the nearest tram stop. There were limits to the amount of walking I could do.

A tram was standing at the stop and I hurried as fast as possible towards it. Suddenly I heard a shout: 'Everybody off!'

I saw that the tram was surrounded by steel-helmeted soldiers who were going through the passengers' parcels and cases.

'Identity cards ready, please.'

I could not turn away, for I knew that the Germans often posted men in civilian clothes on the corners near the place where the 'razzia' – the Belgian name for a full-scale control – was being held. They checked on those who took steps to avoid the control, so the only thing to do was to walk past. I held my hand over the split in the case, the blood pounding in my temples as I walked slowly forward until I was level with the tram. I stared straight ahead of me and kept going. The sweat ran salt on to my tongue as I walked on. I was well past the 'razzia' before I quickened my step. I boarded the tram at the next stop and reached the Place Albert safely.

I met Paul at La Compagne and handed the case over to him.

'You got to Brussels without trouble then?' I asked.

'Oh, yes, but we had to dodge a control at the station. We'll have to watch out; there seem to be a lot more of them just now.'

'You're telling me!'

'I've delivered your set to Michel,' Paul told me. 'We'll meet him tomorrow at noon in the Parc Duden. Same place as before. The sooner you begin sending, the better. There's plenty of work for you to do.'

'I shan't be sorry to start,' I said. 'This hanging about is getting me down.'

'Till tomorrow,' Paul said, holding out his hand.

'Till tomorrow.'

CHAPTER 7

Efforts to Make Contact

As soon as I reached my room, I blacked out the window with my spare blanket and, locking the door, opened my envelope – the one marked 'HILLCAT – PERSONAL'. It contained quite a lot of new instructions which I had to absorb.

I was finishing my coffee the next morning, seated in front of the open window in my room, when I saw two men walking down the cul-de-sac towards our house. I knew all the local people by now and could tell that this couple were not among my neighbours. All the same, there was something familiar about them, or at least about one of them. He was wearing a dark blue suit, an overcoat and a black hat; he carried a small suitcase. Suddenly I realized it was Ping-Pong.

He and his companion came closer and closer. It was impossible that they could be calling on me; as I mentioned, no member of the organization (except for Paul) was told the address of any other unless circumstances made it absolutely necessary. They continued on their way until they were directly under my window, then they crossed the road and the man with Ping-Pong knocked on the door of a house opposite. There was no reply to his knock and after five minutes or so they walked slowly away. It seemed that the organization for which Ping-Pong was to work had found him digs in the same road as mine had for me. Clearly, this was not a very happy arrangement; as I had no intention of moving, I would have to see that Ping-Pong did.

Michel was alone at the meeting which Paul had planned for us in the Parc Duden. Another of his many appointments had prevented him from coming. Michel brought good news: we should be able to go ahead with our first sked on Friday, for he had recruited three young men whom he called Venus, Castor and Pollux, who would help him carry the set and also act as guards during transmissions. They would take it in turns to keep the set at their various homes.

'I've contacted a number of my friends,' he went on, 'and most of them are quite happy to let us use their places.'

'Fine.'

'I'll contact more as we need them.'

'I don't think we ought to return to any house more than once in, say, five weeks, so we'll need about twenty addresses and a few reserves in case of trouble.'

'Right,' Michel smiled.

'Are you likely to be seeing Paul later?' I asked.

'Why?'

I explained about Ping-Pong's unwelcome proximity to me. If Paul could drop some sort of hint about the inadvisability of Ping-Pong staying in the Forest district – without giving any clear reason – I would be grateful. Michel said he would tell Paul.

I myself was contacted by Paul that evening; he had some work he wanted me to do, encoding, so that I would be ready for my sked when it came. The job took longer than I thought; I was very out of practice and it took me over an hour to do one short message.

The next morning Michel told me that be had fixed the sked for a house in Uccle. He and the others would deliver the set there at 3.30. At 3.45 I was to be in the Square Brugmann where I would see and follow him.

On my return to the Léons I checked on the position of the Square Brugmann and found that it would take me half an hour to walk there. It was important to try and gauge these things as accurately as possible, for it was a good security principle not to arrive either early or late for meetings; the less one had to hang about, the less likelihood there was of someone becoming suspicious.

Michel was reading a newspaper as he leaned against a kiosk in the Square centre. As soon as he saw me, he sauntered off and I followed at the same pace as when I had entered the Square. After a short walk he turned in at a gate, crossed a small front garden and entered the house beyond it. As I came up I saw that the door had been left open so I followed on in. Michel was waiting in the hall; a young man was with him.

'*Bonjour, Monsieur*,' I said.

'*Bonjour, Monsieur*.'

We shook hands but did not exchange names, not even faked ones. The young man led the way upstairs and showed me a large bedroom where they had erected a trestle table for me to work on. The houses on the far side of the road were, I observed, set back behind a curtain of trees and there was no danger of being overlooked. I moved the table over under the window where the light was good. I felt a little nervous, more from stage fright than real fear. The young man opened a mahogany cupboard and brought out the set from under a pile of sheets and pillowcases. I had twenty-five minutes until we were due to go on the air. Michel and the young man left me alone to make my arrangements and as a result I felt much less edgy and was able to go about my job with a certain confidence.

But when I tried to make contact, 'We cannot hear you,' was all that I heard.

Paul took our failure better than we had; he seemed almost to expect it.

'Jules couldn't get through yesterday or today,' he told me. 'He could hear Home Station, but they couldn't hear him.'

Michel was having some difficulty finding a suitable house for our next sked.

'First chap was going away for a few days. The second had his mother-in-law staying and she can't stop chattering.'

'What are we going to do?'

'I've found someone, but he's rather scared.'

'Not good,' I commented.

'We have to take what we can get. I don't know the chap personally – he's an elderly man – but I think he's all right. The only thing is that he insists on acting as look-out himself, so you'll have to carry the set. I'll hand it to you at ten-thirty outside the church of the Sacré Coeur. The flat is in the Rue des Patriotes, not far away.' He gave me the exact address. 'After the sked you can meet me at the Café des Quatre Saisons at the corner of the street and I'll take the set back. All right?'

'I suppose so,' I said.

'Oh, and by the way, the old chap insists you have a good cover story ready, so when they answer the door say that you've come to repair the stove.'

I tried to remember everything that Michel had told me and went home to encode the messages which Paul had given me earlier. Our meeting was well-timed the next morning, for Michel and I entered the Rue de Corrège, in which the Sacré Coeur stood, from opposite ends almost simultaneously. He was carrying the wireless in its black box. We stopped and talked for a moment and then shook hands and Michel moved off. He left the box behind and I picked it up and walked away towards the Rue des Patriotes. I ran through my instructions in my head as I walked and found, in a sudden panic, that I could not for the life of me remember the name of the man I was to call on.

Michel would not be returning till just before sked time and I would have to be ready to transmit by then. I tried again to remember, but of course such effort is futile. There were four flats in the building to where I had been directed and as I had some idea that Michel had mentioned the top one, I decided to go there first. I assumed a jaunty air of the kind you might readily associate with a stove repairer and rang the bell. There was no answer until I had tried a second time, then I heard voices within and at last the door was opened a few inches by a woman who was dressed in a flowered smock.

'Come to mend the stove,' I smiled.

'Mend the stove?' she replied. 'Our stove doesn't need mending. There must be some mistake.'

'Well—' I began, but the door was shut before I had time to finish.

There was no reply at flat 3, the next one I rang, nor at number 2. Very clearly it was number 1 on which I should have called. I rang the bell and the door was immediately opened by an old lady with a face of crinkly good humour.

'And what do you want, Monsieur?' she demanded.

'Come to mend the stove,' I said.

'Stove? There's nothing the matter with my stove. Who sent you?'

I was quite taken aback. I did not know the name of any stove repairers. But now my memory was more helpful; I recalled the trade mark on the stove in my room at the Léons.

'Maison Cuppens, Chaussée de Waterloo,' I said.

'Well, I never asked them to send anyone. What was the name and address you were given?'

This was the last question I wished to be asked. 'Frankly,' I said, with a grin which I hoped looked rueful, 'that's just the trouble. The boss gave me the address verbally and he didn't give me the name at all. I'm sure this was the road but I've obviously got the number wrong. I'm very sorry.'

I started to back away.

'You poor thing,' said the old lady. 'I know! Come in and use my telephone. You can get in touch with your boss and get the right address. I hate to think of you tramping up and down the street looking for the right house.'

'Really,' I said, 'there's no need—'

'It's nothing, really. I insist.'

'Unfortunately Madame's kindness will not help me. You see, our telephone has been out of order for two days and they say they can't repair it for another two.'

'Isn't that terrible! I do hope they do something soon.'

'So do I,' I replied, stumbling out of the house.

Smiling fondly after me, she closed the door. I could console myself for the poor show I had made with the thought that I was lucky that there was no one in the house who did in fact need the services of a stove repairer.

It was now 10.30 and I was not due to see Michel again till 11, but I was fortunate enough to see him sitting at a corner café having an aperitif. I hurried up to him.

'What are you doing here?' he demanded.

I explained what had happened.

'It was the top flat. I suppose the old boy got cold feet. What a damn nuisance!'

'Is there anywhere else around here we could use?' I asked desperately.

'I've got some friends quite near,' Michel said, 'but I've never asked them about using their house.'

'Look,' I said, 'H.S. will listen for us for twenty minutes, so that means we've got just over half an hour to get on the air.'

It was ten minutes later when we rang at the house which Michel had suggested, a large mansion in a quiet side street. The people were at home and Michel quickly explained to them what we wanted of them. They hustled us indoors.

'Use any room you want,' the husband said.

I used a large sitting-room on the first floor. I tried all kinds of methods for dealing with electrical difficulties but soon realized that the sked was impossible, so we packed up and left.

I had now been trying to get through to England for a whole week, and on every occasion I had been thwarted by circumstances which, though they were not my fault, were calculated to sap any confidence I had in myself, my equipment, and my mission. I knew how important it was to Paul that I should contact H.S. and I hardly knew how to tell him of our continued failure. He did not blame me (he was too wise a leader for that), but at the same time I saw that he was very worried.

The following Friday I met Michel at a quarter to four on the corner of the Avenue Brugmann and the Avenue de Messidor. We did not speak, but as before he led the way to the place where the sked was to take place: a flat in the Rue des Glaieuls which belonged to a man who was still a prisoner-of-war in Germany. The set was already there.

'Incidentally,' Michel said as we started up the stairs, 'I've told the team that our last two skeds were all right, just to buck them up a bit.'

'Of course,' I said gloomily. 'By the way, is the current O.K. here?'

'A.C. I've checked it.'

'Well, let's hope for better things.'

Michel opened the door of the flat and went in. A kind of damp airlessness filled the place and dust was thick on the furniture and swirled in the sunshafts. A calendar for 1940 hung on the wall. We dared not open the windows, however, for fear of attracting attention.

I rigged up the set. 'We can hear you perfectly – we are ready to take your traffic – over to you.'

'I'm through,' I shouted to Michel. 'They can hear me.'

I started to send. I had included in my messages a request for two extra skeds which would enable me to catch up on all the work I had been prevented from sending. Both these were agreed, one for the next day and one for the day after. We completed the sked and I arranged to meet Michel at 11 the following day (Saturday) for the first of the extra transmissions. Then I dashed off to see Paul.

He was waiting for me near the centre of the city, on the corner by the Zenith café, a wide-fronted affair of chrome and mirrors in which innumerable crystal chandeliers were reflected. German officers thronged the entrance-way; at the back one could see several of them playing billiards with some well-dressed civilians. The Zenith was a haunt of the Germans and their associates.

'That's wonderful news,' Paul said when I had told him of our success. 'Particularly about the extra skeds. I've got two messages I want sent. If we can find somewhere safe to do it I can write them out for you right now.'

'Where do you suggest?' I enquired.

'What about in there?' Paul smiled, pointing to the Zenith. Arm in arm we sauntered through the big glass doors into the brassy interior and found ourselves a table next to a quartet of German subalterns whose table was littered with empty glasses. One of them was trying to make a speech and the others were laughing at his efforts.

Paul took out a large sheet of paper and wrote out the two messages in longhand; they stated quite plainly what they were about, but it was so unthinkable that any but collaborators should use the café that we had not the slightest fear of arousing suspicion. When he had finished, he passed it to me with a flourish and I stuffed it in my pocket, stood up and, shaking hands with Paul, left the café.

Michel told me the next morning that we would be working in a bank. It closed at 12 noon, but the manager often worked on alone and no suspicion would necessarily be aroused by the presence of people on the premises. The manager was waiting for us and took us into the main hall of the building, a large room with a high ceiling and tall frosted-glass windows on two sides. It was difficult to find a way of putting up my apparatus since the only conceivable place to fix it was some sixteen feet from the ground.

'There's a stepladder the cleaners use,' the manager said. 'I'll get that for you.'

I found this very helpful and was able to fix the aerial; I had to keep well away from the windows, however, or people in the street might have noticed someone crawling about on the ceiling of the bark, so we could not turn on a light. I had fifteen minutes left when the time came to plug in to the current; here the trouble was that the lights were hung high in the ceiling, and I decided I would have to make use of the extra yards of flex I had so wisely purchased a few days earlier. I put my hand in my pocket to get it and realized that it was not there; I had left it at home.

'You are a damn fool,' Michel said.

'What shall we do?' the manager asked, more temperate in his language.

I scratched my head. 'I know,' I said, 'I can send from the top of the ladder. This flex will easily reach that far.'

I climbed up, took the bulb from one of the lights and plugged in my adaptor. All was ready.

'Switch on the light,' I ordered.

Michel was about to do so when the manager said, 'Stop! If you switch on you'll turn on all the lights in the row – the one switch works for all of them.'

I scrambled down from the ladder and left Michel and the manager to use it to remove the bulbs from the other lights while I got the set ready. They finished the job and I clambered up with my gear and placed the set on the small platform at the top of the ladder. Swaying slowly back and forth, I tested my keying. I could just about manage. The sked started and I got through all right. My arms were cramped by the unnatural angle at which I was being forced to work and I had to ask for many repetitions when I was sending my second message. When it was acknowledged that they had received it all, they added that they did not think very much of my keying. I am afraid this struck me as rather funny and I set the ladder rocking even more by bursting out laughing.

'What is it?' asked Michel in a rather shocked voice.

'They don't think much of my keying,' I said. 'I wonder how they'd make out at the top of a ruddy ladder!'

I hurried home and set about decoding the message which I had received. They both came out all right – though there were a few gaps in each of them, they were easily resolved. My confidence was now quite restored and I had no doubt about my ability to carry on successfully with my work.

CHAPTER 8

Curfew

The elation of my success soon passed. Exhilaration turned into ennui; transmissions became routine and by so becoming soon lost their excitement. I worked roughly four times a week, arranging skeds at irregular times so that the Germans would find it more difficult to pick up my traffic; they might discover the wavelength on which I was working, but it would need a 24-hour vigil if they wanted to listen in every time I was on the air. My most persistent enemies were interference and atmospherics; there were times when these became so bad that I was forced to postpone the sked. Sometimes Home Station would be unable to hear me and would send their traffic blind, repeating each group so that they could be fairly sure I was getting it down; usually I was able to do so.

As far as the Germans were concerned, their main means of harassing us was by the use of direction-finding units. They tried to break down the signal plans of any illicit transmitters which they heard and, further, by co-ordinating several direction-finding stations they sought to pinpoint the approximate area where the operator was working. They were then able – if he remained on the air long enough – to send out small vans which could locate the operator's whereabouts – if not to the exact house, at least to the block in which he was working. To counteract these vans, we tried to stay on the air for the shortest possible time.

After I had been working for a month the traffic increased so much that we were doing five skeds a week and Michel had some trouble finding enough houses in which to operate. Furthermore, the protection team were overworked and sometimes inclined to be rather edgy. A number of houses and flats which were offered to us proved unsuitable for transmission.

The enthusiasm with which our temporary hosts sometimes greeted us when we called was as embarrassing as it was charming; one could not feel that security was at its best when being introduced to whole families as a British officer. The best-intentioned are not always the least voluble; nevertheless it did not do to forget that the risk they were taking was – were I to be caught in their homes – no less than mine. In order to safeguard them as much as possible I often cut short a sked which I thought had continued too long, even though it entailed not sending or receiving as much traffic as I had intended.

Once I sent from a convent. The Reverend Mother had told her nuns that the electric fire in her room was not working properly and that she had sent for someone to repair it. All the while I was at work she sat beside me reading her Office. When I stopped for a moment, she tapped me on the arm and said, 'Tell them to come quickly and end the suffering of the Belgian people.'

I stared at her for a moment and then nodded and started tapping away as hard as I could go. She smiled contentedly at the promptness with which I obeyed her command.

On another occasion I used the home of an Englishwoman who had married a Belgian after the First World War. She greeted me with the greatest delight.

'I can't wait till after the War when I can tell my husband about this,' she said.

'Why?' I smiled.

'He's a Rexist,[1] you know, and he'll be furious to think we had a British operator using our house. I just can't wait to tell him.'

---

[1] Rexists were members of a political party which favoured collaboration with the Germans.

'Well,' I said, 'in that case I hope you do wait.'

'Look,' she said, 'I'll act as look-out while you're working. All right?'

'Couldn't be better,' I replied.

After the transmission she handed me a list of every soul who had passed the house during that time; she had noted cyclists and motor vehicles as well as mere pedestrians.

'Now, how about a quick one?' she asked.

'Thank you, I could do with it.'

'Shan't be a jiffy,' she cried, hurrying out of the room.

She returned with a bottle of Haig's whisky and a packet of Players cigarettes.

'Here we are,' she said, pouring out two glasses and handing one to me. 'To victory and may it come quickly!'

'Victory!' I cried, raising my glass.

I do not know what the protection team would have thought if they had known that they were guarding a man who was knocking back whisky and smoking Players cigarettes. However, the opportunity was too good to miss. I was even rather excited to be speaking English again (the lady refused to use any other language), and I could not help feeling a little regretful that we did not use her house again.

Early in November I was having one of my routine meetings with Paul and, after concluding our work, we were having a drink when he said, 'By the way, I am going back to England shortly.'

'Oh,' I said, taken aback by the news, 'what's happened?'

'Nothing; it's just time I went back, that's all.'

I was rather shattered; we had been together for a long time and I found him a wonderfully enthusiastic and congenial person with whom to work.

'We shall miss you,' I stammered.

'I'm handing things over to a chap called Victor. We've been working together for some considerable time and he'll be able to take over quite easily. I'll see that you meet him soon.'

The Count had left for England shortly before and Jules, his operator, was due to leave within a couple of weeks; as a result I would have to accept an increased amount of traffic.

'No chance of my getting back, I suppose,' I murmured. 'I've been here for three months myself, you know.'

'I know,' he smiled. 'I'll do what I can about getting someone sent out to take your place.'

'I wish you would,' I replied. 'It would be nice to be home for Christmas.'

In spite of its routine nature, the work was beginning to become very irksome and tiring; my nerves were feeling the strain. I had to work in the afternoons since this was the time which suited the people whose homes we used, which meant that I was often up until late at night decoding the messages for Paul and encoding those he wanted sent to London. I was not sleeping too well. I imagined things. If there was a knock at the door it was enough to set my heart pounding. Controls increased and several times I was searched and my papers examined; luckily no one ever looked in my cuffs or checked my story about working for the railways, but the fear that they would do so next time began to sap my confidence.

During several transmissions I had to stop sending as a result of a danger signal from the protection team. If these were often false alarms, we did not know it at the time. One of our ways of signalling was for a member of the team to blow his nose. One day one of them had a cold and, as he walked round a corner ahead of the man carrying the set, he forgot himself and blew his nose. Instantly we all took evasive action and the sked had to be abandoned.

Another time, a small closed van had driven slowly down the street in which I was transmitting. It passed the house, stopped 50–60 yards further on, then backed up and turned and came back towards me, stopping opposite. I had already stopped sending but it stayed there for a full hour before finally driving off. A week later I was working in the same district when the same small van was seen slowly cruising along a block or two away. Later we heard that two operators had been caught while actually on the air. The Germans announced that both arrests were due to their direction-finding vans; we doubted the truth of this (treachery or sheer bad luck were more likely reasons), but it added to the nervous strain.

Our morale was considerably bolstered by an incident in which I personally had little involvement: the publication of the special edition of the newspaper *Le Soir* by the clandestine press. Many secret publications appeared regularly – *La Libre Belgique* being the oldest and the most consistent – in spite of the Germans' efforts to stamp them out; they were distributed privately and passed on from hand to hand so that, despite the small number of copies, they reached a very wide public. *Le Soir* was the most important daily paper which was openly published and it was, of course, German-controlled. Most people bought it every day because it contained local news of the kind the clandestine papers did not print; the news was written in a ludicrously biased way and you could not believe a word you read. Although the paper was printed in French it was bought by many Germans. The clandestine press planned to produce a counterfeit edition of *Le Soir* on the evening of 11 November 1943, to commemorate the signing of the armistice in 1918. It was to be an exact replica of the collaborating paper – similar in size, in type face, in layout. Most ambitious of all, it was planned to distribute it not in the normal underhand manner but quite openly, by using the newsvendors and kiosks usually devoted to the sale of the genuine *Soir*. This demanded all sorts of risks and split-second timing; if it could be done, however, its effect on morale would be devastating. *Le Soir* was ordinarily distributed about 5 o'clock in the afternoon, by which time there was nearly always a long queue at the various selling points as there were never enough copies available. The plan was to delay the distribution of the genuine edition for half an hour and to circulate the clandestine edition within that time, passing it off as the genuine article. This distribution would need the services of a large number of men if it was to be carried out effectively in the small margin of time they could allow themselves.

A week before the 11th Paul gave me a message to encode and send off; it requested the R.A.F. to arrange for an air-raid warning to be sounded over Brussels at about 4 o'clock on the afternoon of 11 November, and that it should last for a good half-hour. As soon as an air-raid warning sounded the electric power in Brussels was cut off and since the presses of the *Soir* were power-operated this would ensure the edition being delayed. The R.A.F. reply was rather disappointing, though quite justified; they said that they would do as we asked if conditions permitted. This reply made a back-up plan necessary, so it was decided to start a small fire in the garage where the vans which delivered *Le Soir* were parked.

The leading article and the features were written some days in advance and I was able to send a précis of them to London on the 7th. I arranged a sked for 6 o'clock on the 11th, when I could tell them how the whole thing worked out. At 3.30 on that day we waited anxiously to see whether the R.A.F. would be able to make it or not. The day was fine and our hopes were high, but an hour passed and there was no sign of them. The emergency plan was put into effect and worked very well; the vans were sufficiently damaged by the fire for their start to be delayed, and in that time we were able to act.

Just before 5 p.m. I was sitting in a café near the Place Louise and I could see a queue in front of one of the main kiosks where *Le Soir* was usually sold; it grew steadily; civilians and German soldiers joined it and stood waiting patiently.

Time passed. At 5.30 a young man riding a bicycle at great speed, a bundle of papers under one arm, approached the kiosk. He halted and, still holding the papers, explained that the van had broken down and that was why the distribution was being done by bike and there were fewer copies than usual. With that he remounted, flung the papers to the newsvendor and pedalled off at speed. The sale began. Some of the people merely tucked the paper under their arms and walked off. Others unfolded it (it was merely a single full sheet printed on both sides), glanced through the headlines and looked at the pictures. At first sight there was no reason to suspect that it was anything but the genuine article: the opening sentences were only slightly strange, and it was not until you read about a third of the way through a story that you realized it was written with a new slant. Soon those who had loitered were hurrying away to read the paper in secret; more people came dashing up to buy copies and soon the newsvendor was sold out. A minute later the Germans arrived and everyone took to their heels, leaving only the poor kiosk owner protesting he knew nothing.

In a fury, the Germans raced round to the offices of *Le Soir* and arrested numerous journalists, most of them firm collaborators. I heard later that distribution had been as successful elsewhere as in the Place Louise. By that evening everyone in Brussels knew of the substitution, and so eager were they to read the fake edition that copies were selling at as much as 1,000 francs each. When, at 7.30, they switched on to listen to the news in French from London they were able to hear the details of the leading articles which I had transmitted to London a few days earlier. For a brief hour at least, Brussels smiled.

The next afternoon I was due to transmit from a house in Schaerbeeke, a long way from the Léons. I set off well before sked time, which was 5 o'clock, and boarded a tram. Just after 4 an air-raid warning went. The tram stopped (the current was automatically switched off) and for the next 40 minutes two Mosquitos banked and dived and soared over Brussels. They had come exactly 24 hours late. We all had to get off the tram and walk. I could only be grateful that my fellow-passengers did not know that I was responsible for their discomfiture. I blushed to think that perhaps I had requested the raid on the wrong day; it was more likely, however, that there had been a mistake in the decoding at Home Station. My protection team were not in a happy mood when we met; they had had to lug the set for several miles owing to the tram stoppage.

By this time Michel had found an excellent camouflage for my set: a portable radiogram, a beautifully made affair with plated fittings and grey leather covering and handle. When you opened the lid you saw a turntable and a pick-up arm tucked in beside it; a length of flex with a two-pin plug was found in the lid itself. Nothing could have looked more genuine. But by removing four screws the whole turntable could be lifted out and below it, around the electric motor, were the three boxes comprising my set. They were blanketed in thick flannel to prevent their moving about. The pick-up arm came away too and under it were my aerial, the earth wires, my headphones, morse key and extra flex. There was even a space for my pad and pencil, and everything was padded with cotton-wool to avoid its being damaged or making a rattling noise. Of course, if the radiogram had been connected it would not have worked, but it was unlikely that so drastic a check would ever be made. It took longer to pack and unpack the set, but the increased security easily offset this trifling inconvenience.

One evening, a few days before Paul's departure, we had a farewell dinner; Jules, who was also due to leave soon, joined us. We went to L'Epaule de Mouton which was said to be the best restaurant in Brussels. The proprietor himself was the chef and cooked the meals on a large stove which stood in the actual dining-room. He was very proud of the fact that, in spite of their persistence, he had never served any Germans. There were only eight or nine tables in the place and whenever a German requested one he would be informed that they were all booked. On the walls were the signatures of famous people who had dined there in happier days; among them Tom Mix and Charlie Chaplin.

The meal was excellent, its quality scarcely diminished by the shortage of food; the chef's ingenuity compensated for wartime scarcity. After dinner we had brandy and cigars (the latter procured, heaven knows where, by Jules) and would have stayed all evening were it not that Paul was keen to visit some friends of his who had a small ciné-projector on which we could run through the propaganda films we had received from the first drop at Hatrival. The bill was settled (about £5 a head) and having found a taxi, we set out for Paul's friends' place somewhere near L'Observatoire.

There were a large number of people there, most of whom we knew by sight. The projector did not work very well and we saw only spasmodic flashes of the film. I felt rather apprehensive about the whole affair; it was reasonably certain that those who were present needed no encouragement to be patriotic and that propaganda of the scrappy kind we were seeing would hardly serve to increase their enthusiasm, while if the Gestapo were to call they would have the kind of catch they might have dreamed of. Nothing of this kind happened, however, and we drank and chatted till suddenly I realized that it was nearly 10.30. Paul, Jules and I hurried out into the night and just scrambled on the last tram back to the centre of the town; it took Paul and Jules to where they lived, but I had to get off at the Place Van der Kinder (the nearest it went to the Léons) and that left me with a good quarter of an hour's walk. It was ten to eleven when I alighted from the tram; curfew was at 11 p.m.

I had heard that the Germans often stopped people just before curfew if they happened to be in the streets, and checked their identity cards to see whether they would be home by 11; if the address on the card suggested that this was impossible the future offenders would be arrested at once, lest they be missed later. The address on my card (that of the good M. de Nys) was in Schaerbeeke, a long way from my actual destination, and there was no chance of my being able to reach it (even if I were going in the right direction) within nine minutes. I hurried, trying not to seem to do so, through the deserted streets; my shortest way was through the Parc de St Gille, but in order to reach it I should have to pass in front of a poste de gendarmes. I decided to risk it. As I neared the station I saw that there was a gendarme at the door. Now usually one could trust the Gendarmerie, but for this very reason the Germans had started to infiltrate a certain number of Rexists and collaborators into the police in an effort to subvert their loyalty. As I approached I affected to saunter along as though within easy reach of my home. I passed the door . . .

'Hey, you! Do you know what time it is?'

'Certainly,' I replied, without stopping, as though I were answering a genuine question about the time. 'Certainly. It's just five minutes to eleven.'

'You're sure you can get home in five minutes?'

'Easily,' I said. 'Still, perhaps I'd better get a bit of a move on.' With that I set off at a pace which would not have disgraced an Olympic runner. I ran and ran, through the Parc de St Gille and into the Parc Duden.

A clock struck 11, and I slowed down; caution was now more important than speed. I left the park and crept along through the darkened streets (how bright the lamps seemed!) up towards the narrow steel bridge which crossed the railway lines. The bridge was as bare as a skeleton, no cover at all, and a street lamp shone like a spotlight on the bare pavement beyond. A train panted in the goods yard; shunting trucks clanked. Head down, knees bent, I crept beside the low handrail of the bridge and ducked away from and under the lamp; I edged over to the left under the shelter of a wooden fence and moved more confidently forward. I was only 20 yards from the corner of my road when I heard the crunch of heavy boots ahead of me. As I stopped and stood like a black shadow against the fence, a match flared up in the darkness and a cigarette glowed. The footsteps came on towards me and I edged back along the fence, feeling it behind my back with my hands; many of the slats had been taken for firewood and soon I found a gap large enough to crawl through. I ducked down and squeezed between the boards; a slat caught on my coat and thwacked back against the fence as I pulled myself clear. I froze. Had he heard? I could only wait. The steps came closer, then stopped, then came on again, then stopped. I was crouching now, down against the base of the fence; the man drew level with me and went on along the road. He was up by the lamp now. I lay down and, peering round the bottom of the gap I had come through, managed to take a quick peep along the road. It was a German all right; I could see the shape of his helmet, the rifle slung over his shoulder. There was an army store not far away and it was clear that this fellow was the night sentry there and that he had slipped away for a fag. He turned back towards me; as he came level with me, he jerked the fag-end over the fence and hurried back down the road. I pushed back through the fence and went on home.

CHAPTER 9

Arranging Relief

The next evening I was taken by Paul to meet Victor, his successor. He was a very friendly person with a big, domed head, glasses and a smile which creased his face into a thousand wrinkles. He was single and was a director of a firm of coal merchants. I arranged with him about our meetings, which would probably have to be daily, and he gave me the number of his firm so that I could get in touch at short notice.

'That's all there is to do then,' I said.

'I hope it works out all right,' said Paul. 'I don't like to trust you two on your own,' he added, smiling.

I stood up and held out my hand, suddenly a little sad. Paul took it.

'Goodbye,' I said. 'I hope you get back safely.'

'I will,' he replied. 'And the first thing I'm going to do is see about getting you replaced.'

I shook his hand again and walked away. Three weeks later, at the beginning of December, I heard from London that he had arrived safely; he had had to go through France and Spain and into Portugal.

The pressure of work was increasing steadily. Jules, the other operator in our group, had left for Paris and I had to deal with his work as well as my own. Victor and I got on well together and it was thanks to him that I was able to get a consignment of black market coal to fill my stove; I needed it badly, since I was often up half the night decoding or coding various messages, and it was now mid-winter.

In the first week of December we had another successful drop on our landing ground at Hatrival (I have not enumerated any except the first, but we had been using the ground for drops for the last two months or so) and there were three pairs of pigeons in the delivery. The next evening Victor handed me two foolscap sheets covered in single-spaced typing which he wanted me to encode; the arrival of the pigeons made it possible to send back a large volume of correspondence to England at one time, and it was I who had to prepare it. It was 5 in the afternoon when I arrived home and started work and, with the exception of a short break for supper, I worked continuously till 1 o'clock in the morning. When I had encoded all that Victor had written, there still remained the job of copying the messages in their coded form on to the small, flimsy sheets of rice paper which the pigeons would carry to England. Further, both pigeons of the pair carried the same message – lest one be lost – and so I had to copy out all that I had done twice (carbon paper not giving a sufficiently clear copy). All coded material was written in capital letters, and when I finished the job I worked out that I had written about 20,000 of them during the course of my work. It took more rice paper than two pigeons could carry, and we had to use four of them. This left one pair and Victor decided that the sooner we make use of it the better; the longer you leave the pigeons idle, the more acclimatized they become and the less likely they are to bother to go home. So I was at it again the next night; this time I not only had the pigeons' messages to do but also a certain number of ordinary wireless messages to prepare for my next sked. I was encoding for another stretch of six hours; by the end of it, my eyes were sore and red and the capital letters were dancing about like the print of a book if one is trying to read in a fast-moving car.

On 8 December a message came through addressed personally to me. It read:

IMPOSSIBLE SEND OPERATOR TO TAKE OVER STOP RECRUIT LOCALLY AND SEND DETAILS STOP OBTAIN

O.K. FROM US ON HIS SENDING BEFORE INSTRUCT PROCEDURE PLAN AND CODES STOP

I pursed my lips with annoyance; it seemed to me rather unfair to expect me to find someone on the spot and train him before I was allowed to go home. After all, I had been in Brussels a month longer than I had been told I would be; it was time I was allowed to go home, and that was all there was to it. Later I heard that a plane had actually set out a few days before I received my message, had had to turn back owing to bad weather and had crashed on landing; two of the four operators in it had been killed and the others were badly hurt. Wireless operators were not easy to come by and this last misadventure explained why my term had had to be lengthened. I spoke to Victor about the question of recruiting an operator locally and he promised to do his best to find someone who knew morse.

It was at this time that I had to make a change in my protection team. Venus, one of my first helpers, was ill and Castor and Pollux felt that they could not spare the time now that I was working every day; they received no pay for their dangerous work, and had to earn a living as well. Victor said he would get in touch with the team which had worked for Jules; they were all working-class men and could be paid out of our funds. In the meantime, Michel and I pressed on alone.

It was hard and tedious work, and at times unutterably boring; encoding was the dreariest of homework and transmission flat and unrewarding, enlivened only by the danger of discovery. Michel and I walked through the cold, damp streets of the grey city, carrying the set, visiting now this and now that quarter, knocking at closed doors, sometimes being unanswered, transmitting in drab little sitting-rooms, in chill offices, in garrets, in basements; always we were watched by nervous householders, pursued by anxious questions and harassed by the methodical Germans.

At one of our meetings Victor told me that he had found the perfect man to take over from me, but that he would not be available for a week or so; furthermore, he had arranged a meeting with Le Sanglier, the head of Jules' protection team. Le Sanglier was a great bull of a fellow, about 50, with a booming laugh and a ready smile. He always called me Monsieur Felix, despite any protests I might make against this unnecessary formality. Le Sanglier had innumerable friends and relations, and he never had any difficulty in finding houses from which to transmit; it might be a café near the Bourse, a grocer's in Ruysbroock, in the suburbs, or a garage in La Petite Espinet near Waterloo. This variety was excellent for security, but less agreeable from the point of view of travel; I often had to go on an hour's journey to the sked point, and this led to late-night coding sessions. The number of controls was increasing too; on one occasion I was stopped three times while going from the Gare du Nord to the Gare du Midi. At the time I had five messages tucked in my shirt-sleeves, but the search was for bulky objects and firearms in particular and the Germans were so jaundiced with the continual checks that they searched only in the most cursory way – a pat here and a pat there, and then I was on the way again.

Le Sanglier was a strong man and often carried the set himself without bothering to use the rest of the team; he disliked the radio-gram camouflage which we had taken such trouble to obtain. 'Too ruddy heavy,' was his comment. He carried the set in a plain suit-case. When first I opened this I found a .45 service automatic inside.

'You must be mad,' I said, 'carrying a thing like that. The controls are using thirty men these days. You don't stand a chance of shoot-ing your way out.'

'You will excuse me, Monsieur Felix,' he replied in a dignified manner, 'but I do not intend to use the pistol for that purpose. If we are caught while transmitting I intend, with your permission, to shoot first you and then myself.'

'I see,' I said. 'Well, don't be too quick on the trigger, will you?'

'I will try not to be, Monsieur Felix.'

Le Sanglier had one habit which afforded me considerable annoy-ance; he insisted on referring to the set as 'the wireless set'. It seemed to give him the greatest pleasure to shout out this phrase in his booming voice whenever we met in a crowded café or a busy street.

'Look,' I said, 'you really must be more careful. Why don't you refer to the "sewing machine" instead?'

He looked puzzled, then he cried, 'Sapristi! That's a brilliant idea. Sewing machine, eh? That'll fox 'em. Sewing machine.'

He could hardly wait to tell the rest of the team about the new code name we had decided to use. A few hours later we were due to meet for a sked. I was waiting as he approached me, carrying the set. As he saw me, he held it up, his face beaming, and called, 'I've got the sewing machine, but I can't find the blasted aerial anywhere!'

Shortly afterwards, I met Victor at a café in the centre of town. He was accompanied by a young man.

'This is Jefke,' he said, introducing the stranger to me, 'and I think he's just the man we're looking for.'

'I'm very glad to meet you,' I said, sitting down.

He nodded stiffly and unsmilingly. 'Thank you,' he said.

'Jefke,' Victor put in, 'was in the merchant navy before the war as a wireless operator.'

'Couldn't be better.'

'He knows morse perfectly.'

'Our usual speed is about twenty words a minute,' I said.

'I used to work at about thirty-five,' he said, a slow smile flitting across his face. 'I think I can manage twenty.'

'I'll clear it with London,' I told him, 'but you can have a go at the set anyway so that you're familiar with it.'

He joined Le Sanglier and me the next day and watched me as I worked on the sked. I told London that when I tapped out the figures 312 it would mean that I was handing over the key to the new man. The next day I received a message that I should put Jefke on the air. A day later Jefke again joined us.

'I'll send the first message,' I told him, 'and then you can take over.'

'Very well.'

When the sked started I sent out the first groups and then tapped out 312 and signalled to Jefke. He took over; the new operator was on the air. I realized at once that he was first rate and that we need look no further for my replacement. We both took down the incoming traffic, each using one earphone, and he had fewer mistakes than I had.

The next day I had a message from Home Station:

JEFKE'S SENDING PERFECT STOP INSTRUCT HIM IN PROCEDURE AND HILLCAT PLAN STOP SENDING DETAILS YOUR RETURN JOURNEY SOON STOP

It was the first piece of good news I had had for a long time – the first inkling of the possibility of a return to England and to my wife. I took Jefke with me on every sked after this and soon he was able to do the whole job himself, setting up the aerial, establishing contact, sending and receiving. A few days later I was told by London to instruct Jefke in the codes. When he was ready to take over I was to tell them, and they would immediately send me my instructions for returning. I was as good as home, I thought.

I now set about instructing Jefke in the codes. He was very quick-witted and luckily my codes were not as difficult to understand as some others. I met one operator who never managed to master his signal plan at all.

'Well,' I said, after one session, 'how do you feel about it?'

'I'm ready to start,' he said quietly.

'When?' I asked.

'I've got some personal things to sort out,' he replied. 'Would it be all right if I started just after Christmas?'

'We can leave it a few days longer than that if you like.'

At length we decided on 9 January as the day when he would assume control. I said I would leave a week later so that we could meet every day for the first week when he was doing solo skeds, and he could tell me if anything was wrong and whether he needed any help. I sent a message to Home Station to this effect and they replied that they would let me have instructions for my return early in January. The reason for this delay was not that they thought I would leave too soon, but rather that there was less risk of my walking into a trap if they left sending details of the escape route I was to take until just before I was due to depart.

I felt like a schoolboy who senses the end of term actually approaching after a time that has seemed endless. It was as though the holidays had already begun – until London sent over some more pigeons and I had to stay up encoding Victor's messages for them to take back. One night I never got to bed at all.

Christmas was near. The shops were full of gaudy goods which looked very enticing until you saw how much was being asked for them. Only the Germans could afford to buy anything. You saw them walking along with parcels under their arms, staring in the windows which the Belgians passed without a glance.

One day late in December Le Sanglier took me to work in a house near the Gare du Midi. His friends were a couple who lived in a single room in an attic. There was nothing very memorable about this sked except that it was the first and, I think, the only occasion when the operator at Home Station lost her temper with me. I can hardly find it in me to blame her.

In order fully to appreciate our contretemps one must bear in mind that the only means of communication available to us, operator to operator, was a code which was a series of set questions to which there were equally set answers. This time I repeatedly had to ask her to send parts of the messages again, yet to enquiries as to reception at my end I could reply only that everything was perfect!

I could hardly be surprised at her annoyance therefore; her final signing-off signal might have been sent with the aid of a sledgehammer. Perhaps she thought I was being deliberately obstreperous, but this was not the case. The explanation is that the people whose attic we were using had just bought a large live cock for their Christmas dinner and, living in one room, had nowhere to keep it except in with them. All the while I was trying to take down London's message the cock had been crowing with ear-splitting abandon. It was an unsettling *obbligato*. Of course I had to tell London to send as quickly as possible, for I wanted to get down as much as I could between crows. There was – and here was my difficulty – no signal in the code for saying, 'There is a cock shrieking in my ear.'

Just before Christmas we had a run of bad luck. There were two days when skeds went very badly and neither Home Station nor I were able to receive each other's traffic owing to atmospherics. At the next sked I had been on the air for half an hour, with conditions still very bad but just possible, when we had a danger signal from one of the protection team and had to ask H.S. to wait while I went off the air. A small closed van had driven slowly down the street and stopped a short distance away. Conditions were so bad that I had already been on the air long enough for the Germans to be dogging us. We had to wait for them to go. It was an hour and ten minutes later before it slowly drove off. Of course, the sked was ruined.

The next day was Christmas Eve and Le Sanglier had asked me to go to dinner at his place. I knew that there would be a large crowd there and I had refused when he first asked me. However, he was so disappointed that finally I had accepted. I had a sked on the morning of Christmas Eve, but it was not very successful, though I did manage to make some sort of contact. Instead of sending six messages, however, I was able to transmit only two and I received only one from Home Station. I had lunch with Victor immediately after this disappointment and he gave me a further batch of five messages which he wanted sent. Clearly most of Christmas Day would be spent on the air.

I spent all afternoon coding Victor's messages. I must have been very tired, for I destroyed my in-going code sheet in error and was aghast as I realized I would be unable to decode the next five messages from London. I encoded another message, explaining this, to be sent at the first sked on Christmas Day; by the second sked London should have decoded this and know they must send in the earlier code.

The party at Le Sanglier's was bigger than I ever imagined. There were some fifteen people there and by the time I arrived they had already emptied a fair number of bottles; I was greeted with loud cheers and a number of full glasses were held out to me. After several rounds of drinks (all of which I was mindful enough of security to avoid swallowing) we went in to dinner. They must have been saving for a great many weeks to be able to afford so copious a spread; we ate continuously for two hours, yet food was almost unobtainable save on the black market. To have acquired so much meat and so great a supply of vegetables must have meant hours of queueing and weeks of saving. It was as though, for one brief day, freedom had returned; all tongues were loosened and all faces smiled. I felt both tremendously happy and bitterly sad.

Le Sanglier thumped his great fist against the long table and cried, 'Silence, everyone, silence!'

Conversation jerked to a stop as Le Sanglier rose to his feet.

'I should now like to request you, my friends—' (Bravo!) 'to drink the health of our great friend and ally, England' (Cheers). 'England – and to the health of her representative in this room – Monsieur Felix!'

The loudest and most heartfelt of cheers greeted this speech and the whole company rose to their feet, raised their glasses and, turning to me, cried as they drank: 'To England – our friend and our ally!' They put down their glasses and, in the silence which followed, every eye was upon me. There was a lump in my throat as I rose slowly to my feet and smiled nervously round at everyone. A strange earnestness possessed them, as though I was some kind of prophet who might have great news for them. I had none. All I could say was this:

My friends, what Le Sanglier has said and the toast you have just drunk moves me more than I can or will try to say. My friends, Belgium is today overrun by a hateful tyrant, but though she may be in chains her spirit is undefeated and her resistance unquenched. So long as we have people like Le Sanglier among us we may be sure that it never will be. Final victory and freedom will be ours!

104

One more thing I would like to say. When I eventually return to England – in spite of your wonderful hospitality I still hope to get back one day – I shall ask them to let you know that I have arrived safely by broadcasting the following message: '*Le Sanglier et le Chat Sauvage seront toujours bons amis.*'

Vive la Belgique, vive l'Angleterre!

I sat down. So enthusiastically was my speech received that I could only be grateful that the room where we were sitting was at the back of the house; otherwise the noise would have fetched every inquisitive German in the neighbourhood.

On Christmas morning I went to an early mass before meeting Le Sanglier and Marcel, another member of our team. We went to a place called La Hulpe which was a short way out of Brussels and fairly safe from direction-finding; this meant that we could have a good long sked with little fear of interruption. The sked had been arranged at a farm and when we arrived and were introduced to the farmer, I was surprised to have him turn to me and say in English, 'Very glad to have you here. I hope everything will be O.K. for you.'

Naturally enough I said, 'You speak very good English.'

'I ought to,' he replied. 'I'm Canadian by birth. I settled in Belgium after the First War, been here ever since. Married one of the locals, you know.'

'I see.'

'I expect you'd like some beer, wouldn't you?'

'Certainly would,' I smiled.

Soon it was time to start the sked; there was so much traffic that it was of the greatest importance that it should be a success. To my joy the contact proved excellent; all my messages were sent and acknowledged, including the one telling them about the destruction of the codes. When I had finished they told me that they had five messages for me. I said that I could not accept them. They repeated their request to be allowed to send them, but once again I replied that I was unable to take them. It was rather pointless to receive messages that I was incapable of decoding. Nevertheless I blushed when I thought how Home Station would react when, on decoding my messages, they realized that they would have to re-encode all theirs.

My afternoon contact was as perfect as the earlier one, and within fifteen minutes I had taken all five of the messages which I had refused to accept in the morning. I also arranged two skeds a day for the next five days so that I would be able to hand over to Jefke without leaving him a lot of extra work of my own to do. As soon as the sked was over I hurried back to Brussels in order to begin decoding; I was to see Victor in the evening and wanted to have it all done by then. I locked myself in my room and got out my code sheet number 3. When I checked the code group of the first message I found that it did not tally, as it should have done, with the top line of the code sheet. It did not agree. I checked the second message and the second line of the code sheet. That did not agree either. It was not worth going on; what had happened was quite clear. Home Station had not bothered to decode the message I had sent in the morning and had simply set aside the messages I had refused then and sent them in the after-noon. I presumed that this had only happened because they were short-staffed at Christmas.

Normally my messages would be handed on to a decoder as they came in and would often be decoded by the time I had finished the sked. However, I was in no mood to make excuses for the people in England; Le Sanglier, Marcel and I had been risking our lives taking messages which we could not decode and which England would have known we could not decode if they had taken the trouble to find out. I composed a message to this effect for my next sked; so viciously was it worded, however, that in the event I neglected to send it and substituted a milder one. After all, it was Christmas, a fact which was most amply demonstrated by the number of encounters we had during the next two days with those who were suffering the effects of over-indulgence. Our sked the next morning nearly had to be abandoned owing to a hangover; the man in whose house we were to work refused to open up because he was sleeping off his Christmas dinner, and it was only after the fiercest battering on the door that we prevailed upon him to admit us. I think something of the same spirit must have infected Home Station, for two or three days later they mistook me for another operator and, although I sent four messages, they failed to decode any of them because, of course, they tried to do so according to this other operator's code sheet. I was forced to send all four messages again at a subsequent sked.

These things were but the minor nuisances of our business and were quite understandable when viewed dispassionately; nevertheless, to have Home Station make a mistake always seemed the more serious, the less forgivable, in that they were working in safety while we might pay with our lives for their slightest carelessness. Considering the number of operators whose messages they received, their efficiency was of course remarkable, but when one is working in secret and death is synonymous with discovery, one does not consider such points.

CHAPTER 10

The Trap Springs

Though I scarcely dared to think of it, 9 January – the day when I was due to begin the journey home – was slowly approaching. It was only something over four months since I had landed in Belgium, yet time was not reckoned by months when working in enemy territory. What counted was that I had not relaxed for a single moment during my waking hours, that I had worked every day since my arrival and that I had hardly ever had more than five or six hours' sleep in one night. My eyesight (never strong) was feeling the effect of incessant use, often in poor light, and for prolonged periods. I was tense and deadly tired and the strain grew daily greater.

It was at about this time that the Germans instituted a new kind of control which added to our worries; instead of the large squads of 20–30 men which were easy to spot and to avoid, they started using small groups of four or five who hid in doorways and pounced when least expected. Quislings were often used for this work and their command of French made them less easy to satisfy with poor or out-of-date papers. In addition, the hatred in which they were held by the majority of their compatriots made them the more vindictive: what to the German was a mere routine, to the Quisling was a mission. I was netted three times in a week in one of these traps, and I found it very unnerving, though I managed on each occasion to pass on unscathed. But I was lucky, for the rumour was that the Germans had succeeded in making many more arrests than ever before; the story was that whole groups of the Resistance had been rounded up. We were all very edgy. The man said to be responsible for the arrests was one De Zitter, a man of legendary cunning and resource who was supposed to have done more damage to the Resistance in the occupied countries than any other German. I remember we were all given photographs of him with instructions that if we saw him, he was to be killed, whatever the cost. He was a master of disguise, it was said, and could impersonate all kinds of people: further, he spoke English without any accent and so could easily pass as an escaped prisoner-of-war or an agent. He had great charm and personality. In short, he was a grave menace and might strike anywhere and at any time; the mere mention of his presence was enough to create suspicion and fear among our helpers, and this was the worst kind of atmosphere in which to work from the angle of both efficiency and security. De Zitter, in spite of his proficiency at disguise, was detectable by one thing: the little finger of his left hand had been amputated.

A week after De Zitter's supposed arrival in Brussels we heard that he had just succeeded in rounding up a whole organization of the Underground, about 100 people in all. He had so impressed the leader of the organization – a man whom I had met only a few days earlier – that he had been admitted to a position of the greatest trust from which he had been able to betray everyone. It might seem unlikely that, with the elaborate security measures we employed, anyone could penetrate our organizations; on the whole this was true, but there were times when a man would turn up without credentials who, by force of his personality or the plausibility of his story, had to be accepted for what he said he was rather than for what he was known to be. He might say he was a fugitive or a messenger, and in either event it was difficult to reject him. Apparently De Zitter had been believed and, by biding his time, he had succeeded in giving away the whole set-up. This was typical of the man, for he was never concerned with the apprehension of single members of a group.

Passing himself off as a British agent, he would infiltrate the whole organization, so getting to know the top men and, incidentally, those who worked for them. Then he would arrange for the Gestapo to strike simultaneously at every member of the group so that there was no time for any alarm to be given. Sometimes the Germans would allow the organization to continue operating and so would be able to intercept all the messages which were sent to and from London. Eventually, however, we would begin to realize that something was wrong and we would start trying to trace the leak. It was at this point that the Germans usually saw there was nothing further to be gained from allowing the group to continue work, and so would round up all its members. It was a ceaseless game of bluff and double-bluff.

The strange thing about De Zitter was that we were never certain whether he really existed at all; it was always possible that he was a fiction of German counter-espionage. The stories which were told about him were certainly fanciful enough for it to be clear that at least some of his characteristics were fictional. For instance, it was said that he slept in his coffin and that he never undressed. This, however, could scarcely be held to disprove his existence. What seems to me to cast the greatest doubt upon it is the story about his little finger being missing. This may seem implausible, but it is significant, I think, that the sinister villain of John Buchan's *Thirty-Nine Steps* had almost precisely the same qualities, no less than the same deformity as De Zitter. Indeed, save for the different name they are almost identical. Further, after the War no trace was ever found of De Zitter, though perhaps so clever a person would have evaded capture in any case.

I saw Jefke on 6 January and he told me that he was ready to take over. I said I would accompany him on his next two skeds just to make sure that everything was all right and then, on the evening of the 8th, I would give him all my codes and he would take over completely. From then on I would be a mere spectator. Le Sanglier and his friends would act as protection team for Jefke as they had done for me. The ends were tying up and I felt I was as good as on my way.

Just before I was ready to hand over I had a message from London giving me the address of a contact house in Paris; they would confirm that it was still safe a few days before my departure. So I was to go by way of Paris. I would have my final meeting with Jefke to make sure that he was getting through the work without difficulty on the 15th, and I should be free to start for home by the 20th or so.

The next evening (7 January) I had a meeting with Victor and Jefke at the Place Eugène Flagy. Victor was waiting for me.

'Good evening,' he said, as I strolled up.

'Good evening,' I said. 'Everything all right?'

'I think so,' he smiled. 'Sit down and have a drink.'

We ordered aperitifs. 'What's new?' I asked.

'Oh, I'm glad you asked. I've arranged for Jefke, you and I to meet every evening for the next week, just to make sure everything's going smoothly.'

'Right,' I said.

At this moment Jefke arrived. We all shook hands and he sat down at the small tile-topped table with us.

'How did it go?' we asked him.

'Splendidly,' he grinned. 'I finished all the messages in a quarter of an hour.'

'No trouble?' I enquired.

'None.'

'About the new messages—' Victor began.

I took my leave, for there was nothing I could do to help now, then went back to my room and started to assemble my kit for the trip home. I washed my clothes and mended my socks. I saw Victor and Jefke every evening for the next three days, as we had arranged, each time in a different café. On Tuesday Victor told me that he had arranged for me to meet a member of the escape line to Paris on the 16th.

'You'll need a couple of passport photos so that they can get some French papers ready for you. London will send a final O.K. for your

contact address in Paris on the fifteenth. Jefke here can pass you the
O.K. when he sees you then.'

I grinned at Jefke and he smiled back, rather wistfully. When I
reached home I slit open the partition in my writing case where I had
stored my French money and counted it. I had 45,000 francs, which
in those days was quite a lot of money. I also had a number of Swiss
francs and Spanish pesetas. I had learnt my contact address in Paris
by heart and I knew the password and the reply I should expect to
be given. I was to say: *'Je viens de la part de Mademoiselle Jeanne.'* At
the same time I was to unbutton the top button of my overcoat. My
contact would reply: *'Vous voulez dire Mademoiselle Jeanne Dupuis?'*
And he would take a handkerchief from his top pocket. I checked the
top button of my overcoat to make sure that it would last till I got
to Paris. As jittery and excited as a small boy, I prayed that nothing
would happen to stop me going.

At 8 o'clock the next evening we were to meet again at the café in
the Place Eugène Flagy. Victor and I arrived together and sat at one
of the tables in the interior. It was a chilly evening, grey and cheer-
less, and we ordered vin chaud, I remember, to try and warm ourselves
up.

'I've got some more news for you from the escape line,' Victor told
me when our drinks arrived.

I listened carefully while he told me the details. I asked a number
of questions and tried to make sure that I had everything absolutely
clear in my mind. Suddenly we heard a clock strike.

'Hullo,' I said, 'it's half-past. Jefke's late.'

We were both silent.

'It's not like him,' Victor murmured.

'Well,' I said, 'he won't be coming now. He's sure to think that we
haven't waited for him.' (It was a rule that we never waited longer
than twenty minutes for anyone.)

'I said I'd be at the Eglise de la Trinité at nine,' Victor said. 'So
we'll see him there.'

But we did not.

'He may have had trouble with the coding. If he had a bad sked he may have been unable to decode what he took down. I know he's still finding that part pretty difficult,' I said.

'Probably,' Victor agreed, 'probably that's what's happened. Anyway I've got an emergency meeting with him tomorrow morning at eight. At Ma Compagne. Will you come along?'

'I'll be there,' I promised.

'I'll wait inside the café. You wait outside. All right?'

I nodded.

I woke at 6 a.m. It was a black morning and heavy clouds hung over the city. I dressed in the darkness. The streets were full of silent people on their way to work. I had to go along the Rue de la Junction in order to reach Ma Compagne. I never much cared for that particular street; on one side of it rose the heavy, black-red walls of the Prison de St Gille and on the other those of the Prison de Forêt. There was not a window along the whole length of the street.

I reached Ma Compagne, which stood on one corner of the cross-roads on a wide boulevard. On all sides cold cobbles stretched away down the empty streets. An occasional cyclist rode past into the bitter wind. It was 8 o'clock. A horse and cart appeared at the far end of the boulevard and moved slowly (the horse with its head hung low) towards me. I said to myself that Jefke must surely come before the cart passed me. I kept turning round suddenly, hoping to see him hurrying up. The cart creaked towards me, came level with me and moved away down the street; I remember the way the horse turned its head aside from the wind as if to look at me once again. The cart disappeared. It was 8.15.

I could see Victor sitting inside the café. The grey clouds began to drop a drizzle on the wide pavement as I paced back and forth and turned up my collar. A man with a hand-cart, a window-cleaner I think, came up and asked me the time. I looked at my watch.

'Twenty-five past eight,' I said.

It was hopeless; I knew it was. At half-past I walked into the café.

'Hullo,' I cried, with what surprise and good humour I could raise, 'you're in here, are you?'

For a moment Victor looked puzzled, then he saw that I was speaking for the benefit of a German soldier who was leaning against the bar sipping a cup of coffee.

'That's what we agreed,' he said quietly. 'Come and have a drink.'

I ordered a coffee and sat down.

'Not a sign,' I said.

Victor just nodded and looked away. We did not speak for several minutes, then he said, 'I'll go and see Michel. He's got a contact in the Gendarmerie who might be able to tell us something. He'll know if they've arrested anyone recently.'

'I suppose that's the best thing,' I said. 'We'd better know the worst. I'll go down to the Bourse. There's a café there which Le Sanglier uses quite a lot. They might have news.'

'Good,' approved Victor. 'I'll see you this afternoon.'

We drank up our coffee and went out into the drizzling rain. I walked down the boulevard, past the empty shops and eventually caught a tram. A little later I arrived at the café. The proprietor was talking to two women at the back whom I recognized at once: they were the wives of Le Sanglier and of Marcel, another member of Jefke's protection team. Marcel's wife was pregnant.

Madame Sanglier came running up to me and caught my arm.

'What news?' she cried. 'What news is there?'

I looked at her for a second and then I said, 'None. I know nothing.'

She let go of my arm and went back to the other woman. They both stood and looked at me without a word.

'When did you last see them?' I asked in a low, controlled voice.

'They left yesterday morning at nine. We haven't seen either of them since,' Marcel's wife said.

We fell silent again. The café owner polished a glass. 'We're making enquiries,' I stammered at last. 'We'll – we'll let you know when there's any news.'

'Thank you, Monsieur Felix,' said Le Sanglier's wife.

'Do you have any idea where they were working yesterday?'

'My husband mentioned Schaerbeeke,' replied the other woman.

'I see. I must go and tell Victor. One of us will come back later and tell you what we've found out.'

'You will, won't you?' they cried.

'I will,' I promised.

I saw Victor at 3 that afternoon in a café in the Chaussée de Waterloo. Michel was with him. They did not smile when they saw me.

'Well?' I said.

'The worst,' Victor replied tersely. 'Three men were arrested at eleven o'clock yesterday morning in a café in Schaerbeeke.'

'That settles it,' I put in. 'Marcel's wife said that they were working there. She heard him say so.'

'They had the set with them,' Michel went on.

'Idiots!' Victor muttered.

'Apparently they tried to fight their way out, but they were overpowered and taken to the St Gille prison. They've raided Jefke's place and arrested his wife.'

A few days later we heard the full story. It was not direction-finding that had caught them but an ordinary control into which they strayed because they were not keeping a careful watch. Their papers had been in order, but they had had the set with them and of course had had to open it. After that there was no hope. Laziness had been responsible for their capture, for it was a security rule that one man should go ahead and watch for controls. Had this been done, our three friends would never have been caught – for their papers, as I said, were in perfect order.

Our first task was to warn anyone whom our friends who had been captured might be tortured into betraying. This was a standard precaution and we did not for one moment think that anyone would talk; nor was our confidence misplaced. Though all three were treated with the most savage brutality none of them revealed anything. Jefke was interrogated and tortured within an hour of his arrest and could have given away our meeting at the Place Eugène

Flagy. He betrayed neither us nor anyone else, though he was 'questioned' for weeks on end. After several weeks he was sent to Dachau; there he was publicly flogged to death. Of Le Sanglier we never heard anything. But we who knew of his hatred for the Germans were sure that nothing would have restrained him from so reviling his captors as to exhaust their patience within a very short time. They probably shot him a few hours after his arrest. Most tragic of all was the fate of Marcel. When the Americans reached Buchenwald he was found, still alive, but so desperately ill from the effects of starvation, disease and German bestiality that, although everything that could be done was done, he died before he could see his wife and child.

When Michel had told his news, we discussed our next step.

'One thing is quite certain,' Victor said, his eye on Michel, 'you must not sleep at home at least for a few nights.'

'Why not?' asked Michel, not altogether surprised.

'Jefke was often round at your place, you know that.'

'I suppose you're right.'

'I'd better go and warn Castor,' I put in. 'Jefke and I used his place several times.'

'Right. I'll go round to André's [the café by the Bourse] and tell them the worst . . .'

'I don't envy you that,' I murmured.

'What has to be done . . .'

'What about you two staying where you are?' Michel interrupted. 'Are you sure you're safe?'

'None of them knew where I lived,' Victor replied.

'Same with me,' I added.

'The next worry is about the codes,' Victor went on. 'You handed them over to him, didn't you?'

'Certainly,' I answered.

'I wonder if the Boches got them.'

'Well, they've searched his house. It's safer to assume they have. They've probably got the signal plan as well.'

'And the set,' said Michel.

'It's obvious they'll try and work skeds with London. We can bank on that.'

'There's only one thing,' I said, 'and that's to get through before them if we can and warn H.S.'

'That's all very well,' said Victor, 'but what are we going to use for a set?'

There was a silence.

'I suppose I shall have to go to Hatrival and get the spare one,' I said at last.

'I've got it,' Victor cried. 'Jules's set!'

'You're right,' I agreed.

'He left it in a flat near the Gare du Nord. I've got the key for it too. Jefke told me he'd arranged skeds for tomorrow at eleven twenty-five and for Sunday at seven minutes past two.'

'Nothing fixed after Sunday, then?' I asked.

'Never mind that,' Victor replied. 'The important thing is to get you on the air by tomorrow. Michel, can you organize a place to work from?'

'Very well.'

'I'll go and get the set—'

'I can, if you want,' I suggested.

'You go back and get a message ready for sending,' Victor ordered. 'You'll have to use your emergency codes. I suppose you remember them all right?'

'I'll manage, but it's pretty complicated.'

'Right. We'll all meet at Ma Compagne at eight-thirty this evening for a progress check. Clear?'

Michel and I nodded and we all went about our various jobs. I took a long detour on the way home to avoid going down the Rue de la Junction.

My emergency code was one which I had constructed before I left England, and which used as its key a poem which I knew well at the time (I have since forgotten it); it was quite simple to start using it, but it was very slow and I was nearly two hours over encoding the following simple, bleak message:

JEFKE AND PROTECTION TEAM ARRESTED ON NINTH STOP HILLCAT SIGNAL PLAN AND CODES PROBABLY IN ENEMY HANDS STOP ALL IN AND OUT MESSAGES SINCE NINTH MAY HAVE BEEN DECODED BY ENEMY STOP

When I arrived at Ma Compagne at 8.30 Victor and Michel were just going inside. I caught them up and we all shook hands and went in together. We sat at a table in a corner but did *not* (as in spy stories) put our heads together and go into a whispered huddle; we lounged back and spoke in our normal voices. I mention this point because it is so often missed by even quite intelligent writers and actors who have never experienced a situation of the kind they are describing or enacting. They will insist on performing the most unsuspicious acts in the most suspicious manner. They turn their coat collars up and pull their hats down, talk out of the sides of their mouths, and generally act in the most idiotic way. When training people to act as agents, one constantly met those who had only to be told they were to behave precisely as if they were on enemy soil for them to go into the most extraordinary contortions! A lot of spies who were caught may well blame the screen and the cheap thriller for their capture. Nature too often imitates bad art.

'I've found a place,' Michel announced. 'The old flat in the Avenue Molière. The set's there already, thanks to Victor. But I'm afraid we can't manage a protection team at such short notice.'

'It can't be helped,' I nodded.

'Castor's trying to get the old team together, but it'll take a few days.'

'Fair enough.'

'Message all ready?' asked Victor.

'All ready.'

'Excellent.'

I left them and started to walk home, suddenly terribly depressed. My work on the coding of the message had somehow occupied my mind, but now I had nothing to do but wait till the morning. Meanwhile my three friends were being submitted to the most unspeakable horrors and I, though only a few hundred yards from where they were imprisoned, could do nothing for them. Those who have never lived under an occupation cannot understand the tragic impotence to which one was victim. You had no rights. The Germans could do what they wished and there was no appeal against them. Let them kill, it was their right; let them torture, it was their right; let them degrade and mutilate the patriot, it was their right; let them rape, pillage, flog, defile, humiliate whom they wished, it was their right. You learned to recognize the position and psychologically adjust to it, but to hear of the arrest of your closest associates – this was a blow hard indeed to accept; you felt not only stricken at their fate but fearful for your own. I was sick in my very soul.

Five minutes before sked time I was ready to go on the air. The flat in the Avenue Molière was, as the reader will have gathered, one that I had used before and the owner was as helpful now as he had been previously. I had no means of calling H.S. of course, nor did I know what call sign they would be using. I decided to try to recognize their call sign by the keying of the operator. Everyone sends morse in a distinctive way and after months of listening to H.S.'s keying I was confident that I would be able to pick it out. Just before sked time I switched on and slowly revolved the tuning dial around H.S.'s frequency. The set was new to me of course, therefore I did not know the exact position. However, almost at once I picked up a call signal which I was sure came from H.S. I sent my emergency call sign followed by 'I have an extremely important message for you.' After sending for about a minute I switched back to 'Receive', but H.S. had stopped transmitting. There was only one explanation: someone else *was*. H.S. was taking down a message from another operator under the impression that it was genuine. Someone was working the other set, the one which had been captured with our friends. Either Jefke had been tortured into using it or one of their own operators was doing so. I did not believe that any torture would force Jefke into using it, but they had arrested his wife. And what they might do to her was not pleasant to think about; he might have given in so as to save her. Meanwhile, I tried everything I could think of to catch the attention of H.S. But though I must have interfered severely with their reception, they paid no heed.

A little later I knew that I had been right in thinking that someone was using the other set, for I heard H.S. acknowledge the receipt of a message and then start to send their own traffic. I went on trying to interrupt until I heard them close down and knew that it was useless to persevere. I was bitterly disappointed and when Michel came into the room my head was in my hands.

'No good?'

I shook my head. 'It's worse than that,' I said, and told him what had happened.

'Well, it isn't your fault,' he said. 'We'll try again tomorrow and hope we'll have better luck.'

'There wasn't anything I could do,' I groaned.

'I know. Look, we'll take the set to my place. I think we may as well work from there tomorrow.'

'Will it be safe, do you think? You remember what Victor said . . .'

'Nothing's happened yet,' he replied. 'Don't you trust Le Sanglier and Marcel and Jefke?'

'I trust them.'

'Well, then.'

Together we carried the set to Michel's house. That afternoon and the night that followed it were agony. I hardly slept at all. I stared at the minute hand on my watch. I tried to read. I checked the coding of my message so that nothing could go wrong that I could possibly avoid. Half an hour before sked time I arrived at Michel's, and five minutes before it I started to send my call sign, hoping that H.S. would be on the beam and pick it up. It was vital to try to get a hearing before the other set started up. I sent for three minutes, the same group again and again. Then, desperate, I broke the strictest of all security rules and started to send in clear (uncoded). At once H.S. replied. They were receiving me; they said that they would accept my traffic. I began to tap out the vital message. As soon as I had finished it I closed down, refusing to accept their traffic since I knew it would probably be taken down by the enemy monitoring service who, of course, could now tune in on us with the greatest ease. In the circumstances I was not sorry that this was so, for the Germans would realize that London had been warned of Jefke's arrest and would no longer persist in their pirating.

Of course I was very relieved at the success of the sked and decided to go round and see Castor in the hope that he would be able to get together a protection team as he had promised Michel. I felt much happier than I had for a day or two and was walking along without much regard for what was happening around me. Then I turned into Castor's road and was swinging along towards his house when suddenly I saw a squad of German soldiers outside it. I turned in my tracks and doubled back to the corner of the road, then bustled away towards some shops which lined the main road. So Castor's house had been raided. Things did not look good.

I walked around in an aimless way and eventually returned to the road where Castor lived. It was deserted. I walked slowly down the opposite pavement until I came level with the house and could see Castor standing in the window looking out into the road. He saw me and waved to me to wait a minute. I halted, nervously. He came out on to the doorstep and called out, 'Hullo, why don't you drop in for a minute?'

I crossed the pavement and went up to him.

'I thought you had some visitors,' I said in a meaning way, glancing over my shoulder.

'Visitors?' He looked puzzled.

'Boches,' I whispered.

'Oh, them! No, that was just a control. They've all gone. Come in, won't you?' We went into the house. 'Well, what's the news?' he asked when we had sat down.

'That's what I'm here to ask you,' I smiled.

'Well, I saw Pollux and he's agreed to start work again. And he's got some woman who's a friend of his to give us a hand.'

'Excellent. Is she all right?'

'Pollux thinks so,' Castor shrugged.

'We're working tomorrow,' I told him and gave the address.

'We'll be there,' he promised.

We shook hands and I left for home. It was a chilly evening, yellow clouds filling the sky, and I had my hands stuffed in my coat pockets and my head sunk down between the upturned lapels of my overcoat. Suddenly a voice cried: 'Halt!'

I looked up to see that I had blundered into a snap-control. There was no chance of evading it, so I shuffled to a stop. I was used to being stopped – everyone who lived in Brussels was – but usually I was released almost at once. This time, however, I was thoroughly searched, my wallet emptied, my papers carefully examined and my pockets turned out. I was interested to note that they did not look in my shirt cuffs; though on this occasion I was not carrying any messages there, it was good to know that they appeared to constitute a safe hiding-place. It is often thought that if you are carrying anything incriminating and are thoroughly searched it is bound to be discovered; theoretically, of course, this is true, but the Germans and their minions soon fell into a routine, like all soldiers, and did their searching in a manner so methodical as to be predictable as well. This made evasion easier.

The next day it was freezing hard. Lines of bright snow slanted past my window as I was dressing. We were working from an unoccupied house whose owner was a friend of Michel's. He had given us permission to use it and had sent us the keys, but at the same time he warned us to be as quiet as we could; he had asked his neighbour to keep an eye on the place while he was away and if he noticed anything suspicious we might find ourselves having to answer questions from the police. However, as it was the only available house we had to take the risk.

We carried the set down the road where the house was and tried to make sure that no one was watching us before we ducked in the portico and let ourselves in. The place was cold and empty.

'Where do you want to work?' Michel asked.

'It's no good in here,' I replied. 'I can't get a good earth connection.'

'Let's see what's through there,' Michel suggested.

We went through to the back of the house and opened a door which led into the bathroom. Here I managed to rig up a good earth, but the place was like a refrigerator. The owner had told us that it would be necessary to switch on the main control for the electricity as he had turned it off before he left. We found it and I pulled the lever down. Of course, this restored the current to the whole house and five minutes later we discovered that someone had left a light on in the hall which was shining out as clearly as if it were a burglar alarm. Michel ran and turned it off.

I had not prepared a message since I first wanted to be sure that the previous one had been decoded. I was delighted not to have to do any sending; my fingers were numb and stiff and I found it difficult to control the key when I sent my signal to establish contact with H.S. I told them I had no traffic for them and back came their reply: that they had some for me. I was excited to hear this, for it meant that my emergency message had been received and understood. I could hardly hold the pencil in my fingers to take down from London, and had to ask for several repetitions before I was able to read the letters which I was writing. This was all the more annoying since I was keen to get out of the house just as quickly as I could. I had not forgotten about the man next door. At last I had H.S.'s message down and I arranged to be in touch with them during the next two days. Michel and I left the house with all speed. Outside we handed over the set to the protection team, and our group melted quickly away.

I was walking home when suddenly I became conscious of someone a few paces behind me. He seemed to have been there for some time. I could not remember when I had first sensed him, but I felt certain that I was being shadowed. There were just the two of us in the street. I headed for a more crowded district and threaded my way hurriedly through the thin crowds. Still I felt the man was behind me. I went into a large, cheap store and wandered round the barren counters – I kept my eyes on the tawdry goods that were on display, not daring to look up. At length I did so and I stared round the shop, but no one was paying any attention to me, nor could I see anyone who vaguely resembled my pursuer. At first I congratulated myself on my escape and then I realized the truth: no one had been following me at all! My nerves were playing me up.

I made for home. Once there, I lay down on my bed and closed my eyes and tried to get a grip on myself. I knew how dangerous it was to become the victim of one's imagination. It led to jumpiness and that, in its turn, to lack of judgment and perhaps arrest. I got up and went to my table, sat down and started to decode the message from H.S. What I read when I had finished restored my confidence to some extent:

YOUR MESSAGE RECEIVED AND UNDERSTOOD STOP JEFKE BEING WORKED BY ENEMY STOP WILL TRY TO SEND NEW OPERATOR TWO WEEKS TIME CAN YOU CARRY ON TILL THEN STOP

At least I had re-established contact and put an end to the other set being worked. That was something.

However, my effort to get a grip on myself was not very successful and I found it hard to get back to work. I could not concentrate. I was listening all the time – to the creaking of the trees in the wind, to the gurgle of water in the pipes, to footsteps as they came down the silent street. I hardly dared go out for fear of being caught in a control; I no longer trusted myself in a situation where self-reliance was vital. I had to keep this secret; to tell the others of my fears would merely be to plant similar feelings in them. I talked silently to myself as I walked along, trying to discipline my mind into ignoring the dangers of which I was so suddenly conscious.

The work piled up and, as the risk of carrying the set was now increased because of the extra controls, we were forced to send from the same house much more frequently than was wise. Often we used the same place twice in a week, whereas in the old days we seldom returned to the same one more than once in six weeks.

CHAPTER 11

I Part from the Léons

My mind was soon taken off my own worries by the news that Michel was under suspicion. We were extremely lucky in having a contact actually in Gestapo headquarters. The information he could safely pass on was of course very limited, but occasionally he would come up with something really useful. His motives were not of the purest; like some of the more astute Germans he was aware that the tide of war was turning and was seeking, by means of his revelations, to create goodwill for himself. Whatever his purpose, his information was invaluable and Michel was immediately dropped from my protection team; he left home and stayed with friends. I put through a message to H.S. asking whether, in view of the circumstances, he might accompany me to England when the time came. This was approved, to the delight of all of us.

A little later came the message that an operator was now ready to be sent over; he would be dropped at the first opportunity during the next moon period which began on 29 January. I restrained my excitement by recalling that we had not had a successful drop on our ground for over three months owing to unsuitable weather.

At the same time as we heard that an operator was to be dropped we were asked by London whether we would be prepared to receive another 'body'; his work was not connected with our organization, but his own had no ground suitable for a drop. We had been asked to receive this particular gentleman (whose name was 'Yapok') before and had agreed on several occasions to do so; each time he had been forced to return to England for some reason or other. Victor now refused to accept 'Yapok' at the same time as the other operator.

'He brings bad luck,' he explained. 'I don't want anything to do with him.'

Victor's superstitious attitude proved to be justified. Another organization accepted 'Yapok' and a week or so later he was dropped. He proved to be a double agent in the pay of the Germans and betrayed the whole of the reception team and many of the members of the organization which had agreed to help him. All were executed. Eventually 'Yapok' fell into the hands of the Resistance. He was made to dig his own grave; then he was shot in the back.

On the evening of 31 January I had a meeting with Victor. I found him in a state of great elation, an elation which I soon shared when he told me that the new operator had been safely dropped.

'He'll be in Brussels tomorrow,' he told me.

'I can hardly believe it.'

'It's true, my friend. I'm afraid I'll have to ask you to do the same with him as you did with – with Jefke.'

'Of course,' I replied.

'It'll only mean a few days. Just until he gets to know the ropes.'

'Right.'

'Incidentally,' Victor smiled, 'I've arranged for you and Michel to meet the forger. He'll be seeing to your papers for the journey.'

The following morning Michel, Victor and I met the forger. A small, bright-eyed man with a matter-of-fact manner, he wore a beret and carried a walking-stick on which he leaned as he spoke.

'We're arranging for you to be residents of the French port of L'Orient. It's been heavily bombed by the Americans recently and there are many homeless. Furthermore, the town hall was completely wrecked and all their records burned. They can't possibly check on the validity of the papers we shall give you.'

Michel and I grinned at each other.

'We can't fix you up with *cartes de travail*, I'm afraid,' continued the forger, 'so you'll have to try and get those for yourselves when you reach France. You can say they were destroyed in the bombing if anyone asks you for them. Anyway, have some occupation you can give them if they question you.'

'Any questions?' asked Victor.

We shook our heads.

'I've been able to get plenty of French francs for you,' Victor said. 'You won't have to worry about money. Did you have any luck getting in touch with the escape line into France?'

'All set,' nodded Michel. 'We go to Tournai first and there's a contact there. I have to show him this five-franc piece and then he'll give us the next address.'

'Excellent.' Victor turned to the forger. 'When do you think you can have the papers ready?' he asked.

'Is tomorrow soon enough?'

That afternoon I had a sked. One of the messages I received was that the address in Paris which I had been given was now useless. The Gestapo had raided the place. If we had left earlier we would have walked straight into a trap. London gave me a new address and a new password. It was sheer luck that we had not yet started on our journey.

In the evening I met Lucien, the new operator. He was young and enthusiastic, and I gave him all the tips I could. We planned that he should go on the air for the first time on 6 February; on the 9th Michel and I would leave for Paris. As I was now on the point of leaving I took a chance and committed a breach of security. I got in touch with an uncle of mine who lived in Brussels and arranged to meet him in the Parc Leopold. It was a strange moment when I saw the figure of my uncle, a small briefcase in his hand, approaching the bench where I sat. He had brought a huge sum of money with him in case I might be in some kind of trouble. I said that I was about to leave for England and wanted to make sure he was all right before I did so. I told him what the message would be on the B.B.C., which would tell our friends that I had arrived safely. There seemed nothing else to say to him and after a few minutes' conversation we parted.

That evening I had a routine meeting with Victor in the Café du Diable in the Chaussée d'Alsenburg. It was a quiet place and, so far as we knew, no one else was aware that we were there. We were at a table at the back of the café, talking quite loudly but with our heads together, when a voice said, 'Excuse me, gentlemen—'

We looked up and blinked. It was Jules, the Count's radio operator who we thought had left Brussels months before.

'May I join you?' he asked, pulling up a chair.

We were so astonished that we just sat and stared at him. Finally I managed to say, 'What are you doing here? We thought you were safe with your mother.'

'I've had a perfectly bloody time,' he replied. 'Then I ran out of cash and – well, here I am.'

'How did you know we were here?' Victor enquired sharply.

'How did I know? I didn't know. I've been in Brussels five days and during that time I've been in every café in town where I thought I might find you. It's just a bit of luck I've found you tonight.'

'You seem to have managed the return trip from France very easily,' Victor went on. 'How did you do it?'

'I've got some wonderful papers. I'm a commercial traveller, which means that I can cross any frontier I like and no questions asked. I crossed in a first-class sleeper this time. That's the way to live.'

Victor raised his eyebrows. 'Indeed. Well, how much money do you want?'

Jules grinned – and named a very large sum.

'That's a great deal of money,' Victor said. 'Why do you need so much?' There was a touch of acid in his voice.

'I've got into debt, my friend. I'd like to repay the people who've helped me before I do anything else.'

'Including the first-class booking clerk?'

Jules grinned again. 'If you can get hold of the money, I can get back to Paris tomorrow.'

'I'll try.'

'I knew I could rely on you.'

The reason for the asperity of Victor's questions to Jules was not that he suspected him of treachery; it was rather that Jules had the reputation of being a man who liked what are called the good things of life. It was always possible that he was being more extravagant with the money given to him than the situation warranted. Anyway, Victor arranged to meet him – with the money – the next morning, and we all went home.

The next morning was quite a landmark in my career; I worked my last sked. At the time I could hardly believe it and told myself not to be too optimistic: the future was too uncertain for anything to be definite. However, Lucien made successful contact at both of his skeds during the following two days, and in that time Michel and I had several meetings when we made plans and discussed tactics for our trip. It was agreed that I should pose as a buyer in a textile firm, this being a trade of which I had some small knowledge.

Now that everything seemed to be going smoothly the time came for me to give notice to the Léons who had looked after me so well during my stay in Brussels. I had been with them for five months and never once had any suspicion fallen upon me, a tribute to their discretion. I bought Monsieur Léon a half kilo of the best tobacco obtainable on the black market, and from the same source a mammoth box of chocolates for Madame. Both of them wept and flung themselves upon me in their delight, at the same time protesting their sorrow at my departure. This was scheduled for 9.30 at the Gare du Midi on the morning of 9 February 1944.

On the evening of the 8th Michel and I had a farewell dinner with Victor. No one could have a better leader. He was as unfailing with praise as he was sparing of criticism and he was always at his best – or appeared to be – at the very moment when one's spirits were lowest. We sat and chatted long into the night, talking of the past and planning for the future. We would all meet and have a tremendous party as soon as the Allies entered Belgium.

This was not to be, however. Two months after I left, Lucien and

Castor were arrested during a transmission. Our organization had been penetrated and Victor received word that he was wanted; he managed to escape before the Gestapo arrived and went into hiding. A few weeks later he took the risk of visiting his parents. It cost him his life; their house was being watched and he was caught. For many weeks he was tortured by the Germans with a brutality that it is now fashionable to forget. He told nothing. When they saw that they could obtain no information from him, the Germans took him out and hanged him.

Lucien and Castor were treated with the same brand of unspeakable cruelty: they were held under in a cold bath, they were beaten with rubber tubing and were interrogated nonstop for hours on end. They were still in the prison of St Gille when the Allied forces were nearing Brussels, but one morning the prisoners were all loaded into cattle trucks for transportation to Germany. The Resistance got wind of the plan and countered it by sabotaging the engine of the train. When that was repaired they blew up several yards of track just outside Brussels. So great was the damage that the Germans gave up the attempt and abandoned the train which the Allies discovered several hours later. The prisoners had been locked in the trucks for two days and when the Red Cross came many were in a state of collapse. At first they refused to leave the train, thinking that the Germans were masquerading as rescuers in order to lure them out and shoot them down. When at last they were convinced, they could hardly believe their good fortune. I am glad to say that Castor and Lucien were among those who made a complete recovery.

CHAPTER 12

Crossing a Frontier

I waited by the entrance of the Gare du Midi, looking for Michel. We were really on our way. In a few minutes he came along and I waved to him cheerily. He came up to me and we shook hands; it was as if we were wishing ourselves luck.

'They've changed the train,' he told me. 'We've got to go over to the Gare du Nord and pick it up there.'

Such changes were common during the War and we were used to them. There was no difficulty about catching the train and the journey, though long and slow, was uneventful. For the purposes of the trip Michel and I pretended to be strangers; should one of us be caught there was no sense in the other being automatically incriminated.

It was getting dark when we reached Tournai, but we easily found the address we had been given. Michel had the five-franc piece by which we were to make ourselves known, so it was he who rang the bell. The door was opened by a middle-aged woman of generous proportions.

'Well?' she demanded.

Michel drew the five-franc piece from his pocket and handed it to her. She glanced at it and then at us.

'Come in.'

Soon we were being served with bread, cheese and coffee.

'Now then,' she said when we had eaten, 'to business. Let me see your French papers.'

She spoke in the tone of a nurse asking to see a patient's tongue. We produced our papers and she examined them.

'Not bad,' was her opinion, 'but they've left out the fingerprints. I'll get my ink-pad and we can attend to that right away.' We did so. 'Now,' she continued, 'about tomorrow. You'll be staying overnight at a house a few doors away; they're elderly people and quite trustworthy. They'll give you *petit déjeuner* at six. Be ready to leave at six-thirty because we have to catch the quarter to seven tram. I'll be waiting near the tram stop – you know the one, on the corner – with my bicycle. Don't on any account speak to me. When the tram comes I'll ride ahead of it and be waiting for you when you get off. I'll then move off and you must follow. Clear?'

'Quite clear,' Michel replied. 'But what about the frontier, will there be any difficulty crossing it?'

'No trouble going out of Belgium,' she said.

'What about getting into France?'

'We'll worry about that when we come to it.'

Michel and I hid our French papers in the inside pockets of our waistcoats, for to be found with French papers in Belgium would be to invite investigation.

It was still dark and bitterly cold when we left our lodgings and made for the tram stop. Our guide, pushing her bicycle, soon arrived but, according to plan, ignored us. The tram was late and we were nearly frozen stiff when it arrived. As it appeared we saw Madame get on to her bicycle and start off down the road. It was some time before the tram caught up with her and some time after that before we reached our destination and got off. It was still quite dark but we were able to follow our guide, leaving some hundred yards between ourselves and her, as she started along the road. The country was flat and open; only the odd tree disturbed the monotony. A cold wind slashed at our faces and frost glinted on the hard ground as we left the road and started down a track. Five or six miles down this track we came to a small wood, where we saw that Madame was waiting for us.

'How much farther to the frontier?' demanded Michel, chafing his hands together and stamping his feet on the ground.

'How much farther? No farther. We've already crossed it,' was the smiling reply. 'We're just about to pass into France. Will you please give me all the Belgian money you've got, and your Belgian papers as well?'

We did as we were told and took our French papers out of hiding, putting them into our wallets.

'Off we go again.'

A few minutes' walk took us to the far side of the wood, where Madame halted again.

'Now then,' she said, 'you see the farmhouse over there. The farmer and his wife are friends of mine and I hope they'll lend me a couple of bikes you can use.'

'Why, what's the plan?' I asked.

'All in good time. Three hundred yards farther up here is the fron-tier post. You can just see the roof over the top of that hedge.' We peered in the direction indicated. 'There's a bar across the main track to stop traffic, but they don't bother to lift it for cyclists as there's a narrow track that runs outside the barrier. All you have to do is pedal as fast as you can down the path and past the post.' She smiled at us as if inviting us to applaud the ingenuity of her ruse. I think we both looked rather glum, for she went on, 'It's quite possible there won't be anyone there and even if there is you should be well past it before the guard sees what's happening. He's got no telephone or anything, so all he can do is shout. Probably he won't bother at all, even if he is there, because there are people going back and forth across the frontier every day all day. All right?'

There was no choice but to agree. Ten minutes later she returned from the farm with the oldest bicycle I have ever seen. It had no mudguards and no brakes; the tyres were stuffed with hay.

'Good news!' she cried cheerfully. 'My friends say they don't think there's anybody in the post at the moment. I'm afraid they only had one bike, so we'd better tie both your cases on to it and one of you can ride across and the other follow on foot. Who's going to take the bike?'

It was agreed that I should.

'Don't worry,' she cried, 'I'll get you across all right.'

We tied the suitcases on to the handlebars and then Madame wheeled her bike on to the road. She would lead, she said, and I was to follow. Our lightning dash began. Her machine was vastly superior to mine and anyway I am not very good on a bicycle; soon I was lagging badly. It was all I could do to keep my balance. Speed was impossible. I do not know what there was on the machine which could rattle, but whatever there was did so. I reckon I was doing well if I was up to six miles an hour when I came wobbling up to the frontier post. I negotiated the narrow track and continued on my uncertain way. No one came to the door of the hut or shouted at me, and I could only assume it was empty. Half a mile farther on the track had a bend in it and when I rounded this I found Madame awaiting me.

'What did I tell you?' she demanded. 'No trouble at all. Now then, do you see those houses over there?'

'Yes,' I replied.

'That's the village of Hergnies. You walk on slowly and wait there. I'm going back to see that your friend is all right.'

I was not going to ride the bicycle again if I could help it, so I started to wheel it along the track. I had not gone more than a few yards when there was a rending noise and my suitcase fell from the handlebars into the road. The handle had split.

There was plenty of time, so I laid the bike on its side and set about making repairs. I was squatting down by the roadside engaged in doing so when I heard the sound of footsteps approaching along the hard path from Hergnies. I glanced up to see a gendarme coming towards me and almost panicked. I could not think of any explanation – not even a humorous one – for the fact that I had two suitcases, each containing pyjamas and toilet things. I was but half a mile along the road which led only from Belgium, yet my papers showed me to be a Frenchman; it would not be easy to explain why I had no passport if

I had only just crossed into France. Further, I suddenly remembered that one needed a permit to ride a bicycle. My mind refused to function; there were too many inconsistencies for me to be able to reconcile them. Meanwhile the gendarme slowly approached.

Perhaps it would be better if I were on the move, I thought; he would be less likely to start a conversation. I tucked my case under my arm, hurriedly grabbed the bike and started walking towards the gendarme. My face relapsed into a silly frozen grin, a kind of imbecile profession of innocence. He did not look at me at all. I came up to him and we passed each other; he never glanced my way. Once past him, I experienced a violent reaction against my earlier panic and wanted desperately to giggle.

Madame and Michel soon caught me up.

'Any trouble?' I asked.

'Post was empty,' Michel replied.

'What about the gendarme though?'

'Didn't even look at us.'

'I expect,' concluded Madame, 'that he was a Frenchman on the run. He was probably terrified you'd ask him a question!'

Madame led us to a house near the outskirts of the village where she received a cordial welcome. We gathered that she had brought innumerable people across the frontier, all by the same simple manner. The people there served us with some food, and as we were finishing it Madame stood up and said, 'Well, I must be going now. I have a long way to go to get home.'

We thanked her for her help and she wished us good luck and departed. When she had gone the owner of the house took over the responsibility for us. He briefed us about the next part of the journey.

'There's a steam tram that leaves Hergnies every few hours,' he told us. 'It will take you as far as Valenciennes. From there you can get a train to Douai. At Douai you pick up the express for Paris. That'll get you to Paris at about ten-thirty.'

'What time is curfew?' I asked.

'Midnight. You won't have a lot of time. Incidentally, the tram is likely to be stopped and searched by the V.N.V. a bit further along the line.'

'V.N.V.?'

'Oh, they're collaborators, so you'll have to watch out. They speak French, unlike the Boches, and so they're likely to ask trickier questions.'

Michel and I caught the tram as planned; it consisted of three carriages which had platforms at each end. It was only about half-full and we had no difficulty in finding seats in the middle carriage. We passed three or four stops without incident and began to hope that the V.N.V. were taking a day off. We were swaying along in the middle of open country when slowly we came to a halt: four members of the V.N.V. were standing in the roadway. I was facing forward, with Michel opposite me, so I saw them pass me and go to the back of the tram. One man, armed with a sub-machine gun, stood on either side of the tram to make sure nobody tried to get out.

From the questions I could hear being asked I could tell that the two remaining men were checking papers, searching parcels and cases. Neither Michel nor I had prepared complete cover stories and now I started to try to think of good answers to the sort of questions we were sure to be asked; from Michel's expression I could tell he was doing the same. I thought I would say that I was homeless after the bombing of L'Orient and I had travelled to Hergnies where an uncle of mine used to live years before. I would say I had discovered that he had left the village at the beginning of the War and no one had any idea where he was. So I was going to Paris to look for work.

In less than five minutes the men had completed their check of the rear carriage and they came through into ours.

The first two men they started to search were workers. They wore blue cotton trousers and heavy sweaters and had greasy old cloth caps on their heads.

'Hurry up,' I heard one of the guards say. 'Get these parcels open.'

Suddenly there was a scuffle and shouting. The two guards in the road closed in, jumped up into the tram and dragged the two workmen off. Their parcels were chucked out after them. My apprehension grew as the four Quislings marched their suspects towards the front of the tram. Then the leader made a sign to the driver and the tram moved off, leaving the V.N.V. men with their prisoners. Michel and I relaxed. At the next stop most of the other passengers got off. We were alone in our part of the carriage.

'A nasty moment,' I commented. 'I hope you had a cover story ready.'

'I made one up,' he said, 'but it wasn't very convincing.'

'What was it?' I asked.

'Well, I thought I'd say that I'd been made homeless by the bombing in L'Orient, so I'd come to Hergnies looking for a relative of mine who used to live here. I'd found he died a few years ago so now I was going to Paris to look for work.'

I was glad that the check had not come as far as our part of the carriage . . .

In Valenciennes we made straight for the railway station to find out about trains. There was nothing advertised on the timetable till nearly 6 o'clock.

'This can't be right,' Michel said. 'We'd better ask someone if there's anything before this.'

We went over to the booking office and asked the clerk.

'Quite right,' he told us, 'nothing till six. And that won't come in until eight if I know anything.'

'But we've got to get to Paris,' I cried.

'Not a chance, not a chance in hell.'

'I don't know what to do,' Michel muttered as we moved off.

'Here, hold on a minute,' called the clerk. 'I've just thought of something. There's a special due in about half an hour. It only runs once every two weeks, but it happens to be due today. It's a German leave train, but civilians are allowed on it.'

'That's splendid,' I cried. 'Our troubles are over.'

He leaned out of his booth towards us and said, 'Not necessarily.

I ought to warn you this train gets blown up with amazing regularity. You travel at your own risk.'

We bought our tickets and went and had a cup of dishwater coffee. When the train came in we found that it was packed with German soldiers, but there were also a number of civilians so we did not feel too conspicuous. We were jammed in the corridor. But Douai was reached without our being harmed by either French saboteurs or German controls. On leaving the train, however, we saw that a very thorough check was being carried out at the barrier.

'This is it,' I whispered.

'It's all right,' Michel replied, 'it's only a military control. They aren't bothering with the civilians.'

The Paris express was not due for half an hour, so we went into the station buffet to try to get a sandwich. But without bread tickets it was impossible; we sat down and waited. The express was nothing like as full as the leave train and though this made it much more comfortable we really preferred the packed trains; they made controls much more difficult to carry out. The train waited a long time at the station and it was after 7 p.m. before it pulled out. As a result it was 11.30 before we steamed into the Gare du Nord. And curfew was at midnight.

'What's the best thing to do?' I asked Michel as we passed the barrier.

'I don't think there's a hope of getting in touch with our contact at this hour, do you?' I shook my head. 'Well, we'd best start looking for a hotel.'

'Let's see if this fellow can help us,' I said, pointing to a station official.

'All right,' Michel agreed.

I asked the man whether he could recommend us a hotel not too far from the station where we could spend the night.

'You'll never get into a hotel,' was the depressing answer, 'and certainly not in the centre of town. Most of 'em have been taken over by the Germans, and the others are always booked up weeks in advance.'

'What about curfew? Is it strictly enforced?'

'I'll say so. Look, the best thing you can do is go to the nearest police station and tell them the position. They'll look after you until the morning.'

We thanked him politely for his advice and walked away. Of course to do as he had proposed – though all right for the ordinary traveller – would be suicidal for us. We approached another official and asked whether we could spend the night in the waiting room.

'Quite impossible,' he said, looking at us sharply. 'There will be a check on all persons in the station after twelve o'clock and everyone must establish that he is waiting for a train or else risk arrest.'

We half-walked, half-trotted out of the station and into the black-out. We had just over twenty minutes to find a bed, or at least shelter, for the night. We were met by a few taxi-drivers who demanded whether they could take us anywhere. Instead of real taxis they were driving ordinary bicycles with a two-seater wicker chair on light wheels fastened on behind. We ignored them and set off into the darkness, not having any idea where we were going.

'Here's a hotel,' I whispered to Michel after we had gone a few hundred yards. 'Let's try it.'

We went in through the swing door and found ourselves in a dimly lit foyer. I pinged the bell on the counter; after a few seconds a woman came out of an inner room.

'We would like a room for the night,' I said boldly.

'You would, would you? And have you booked?'

'No,' I replied. 'But we would be prepared to pay—'

'I'm sorry,' she said curtly and went back into the inner room.

We looked at each other for a moment and hurried out again into the night. We did not even get as far as the foyers of the other hotels in the road; they were already locked up and no one would answer the door when we rang. The streets were quite empty, there was no light. We dashed from door to door, crossed the road and tried the hotels on the other side.

Soon we found ourselves back by the station. It was five to twelve and I felt the sudden breathlessness of despair. Complete silence. Then we heard the crunch-crunch, crunch-crunch of boots marching along towards us. A narrow street, showing like a slice of pitch, branched off to the left; as silently as we could we crept into it. The patrol kept coming and we decided to move farther down the street; they turned into the lane and started down it towards us. We hurried on to where a faint light shone in a doorway – the entrance to a small hotel. We pushed at the door, which fortunately was open, and went in. A weak bulb daubed with blue paint glowed dimly, showing a cold, black stove in the middle of the tiled foyer and around it three armchairs whose rusty springs protruded through the brown seats. Dust was drifted like snow against the cheap brown wood reception desk. There was no one about when we entered and this was as well; we hoped that the patrol would be well past by the time we were ejected.

The patter of slippers on the stairs disturbed the silence. At length an old man appeared; he was in his shirtsleeves and his scraggy arms grasped at the rickety banisters. White stubble covered his sunken cheeks. He stopped suddenly when he saw us, his expression suggesting that he had not heard us come in.

'Well,' he said in a nasty tone, 'who the hell are you?'

'We have just arrived in Paris, Monsieur,' explained Michel. 'We want a room.'

A clock on the mantelpiece struck with twelve tinny chimes.

'Isn't one in the place. Hasn't been for months. Now get out. Go on! I'm just going to lock up.'

We had expected this, but we knew now that we could not go out. There was not a hope of surviving five hours out in the streets with all the German patrols. Michel shrugged.

'Look,' I said, as the *patron* started to motion us outside, 'if you'll let us spend the night in those armchairs we'll pay you the price of a room.'

He stopped and a little smile puckered his face.

'Hm, well, we might be able to arrange something. For about four hundred francs, we might well arrange something.'

He must have thought he was demanding an extortionate price, but if he had asked 4,000 francs we would have paid it cheerfully. All the same, for appearances' sake, I said, 'That's rather steep, isn't it?'

'It's as you wish,' he said in a surly manner.

'Well,' I said, 'it's a lot of money.'

'If I get you a proper room for four-fifty, will that be all right?'

Michel and I pretended to discuss this offer, then agreed to it. The man went over to the reception desk and picked up the house phone.

'Is that you, Monsieur François?' he enquired. 'Ah, good. Now forgive my asking, but is mademoiselle from number twenty-one with you tonight? Ah, thank you, thank you, I want to make use of her room tonight. I'll fix it with her in the morning.' He replaced the receiver and favoured us with a seedy smile. 'It is all arranged, gentlemen. The only thing that remains is for you to fill in the register.'

Michel filled in both names; I left it to him because my handwriting is very English and I did not care to risk it. I handed him my identity card so that he could copy the details from it; however, he could hardly take out his own since all that was required was your name, address and profession. To copy from your own card would be to confess that you did not know these details about yourself! Michel managed to remember nearly everything which was wanted, but he could not recall the name of the road where he was supposed to live.

I was just putting my card away in my pocket when the man said that we must leave them with him until morning. They would be returned to us when we left.

'What's the idea?' I asked.

'The Gestapo calls here early every morning to check on the residents. They always want to see their cards too.'

'You mean they drag you out of bed at the crack of dawn every morning?' Michel cried.

'Any time after six,' was the reply. 'I have to be up by then.'

'I see,' Michel said. 'Well, I'm glad to hear that because we have to be out of here very early to catch a train. In fact, I think it would be a good idea if we settled our account right away.'

We did so. The old man locked our identity cards in a drawer and told us to follow him upstairs. The stairs were covered with worn lino and the stench of urine was everywhere. On the third floor we halted; the man opened the door of room 21 and flicked on the light which cast a dim yellow glow on to the scene. We went in and he left us.

A dirty bedspread was hung over the window as a blackout curtain. The walls were covered with peeling yellow paper on which damp roses spread like a rash. There was a small iron bedstead made up with grey sheets, and beside it a broken chair. The floor was bare save for a greasy piece of carpet in front of the washstand. A trunk stood in one corner. The bed was unmade and this was far from the only evidence of the late tenant's presence; everywhere were old powder boxes, rouge pots, hair-curlers, and slung over the towel-rail were several pairs of silk stockings and a couple of brassières. The wash-basin was half full of soapy water and black hairs floated on it like scum. The place reeked of cheap scent.

'The armchairs might have been a better idea,' Michel remarked.

'Too late now,' I said.

We were both desperately tired, yet the idea of lying in the filthy sheets repelled us. It was so cold that we decided to compromise. We stripped down to our underclothes and then, removing the sheets, wrapped ourselves in the thin grey blankets. I turned out the light and we composed ourselves for sleep.

'Hell!' said Michel suddenly.

'What is it?' I cried.

'I've just remembered I filled in the wrong road in the register. Let's hope he doesn't compare my identity card with what I wrote in his book.'

'That's another good reason for being up and out of here by six,' I said.

Luckily, it was almost impossible to sleep soundly in the bed in which it was as cold as the grave, and each time we woke up we were chilled to the bone. By 5 o'clock we were famished and stiff with cold, at which point we decided to give up any attempt to rest. We got up and I went over to the wash-basin, but the floating hairs soon deterred me from washing. We made the bed and went out on to the landing. Nothing stirred as we crept downstairs. If we could have got at our identity cards we could have left at once, but they were locked up. We waited anxiously for the *patron*. Six o'clock came and went. We coughed and stamped our feet. At a quarter-past a fat woman came up the stairs from the basement.

'What's all the noise about?' she demanded.

'We want our identity cards,' Michel explained. 'We've got a train to catch.'

'Wait here.'

We had little choice but to do so. The woman went upstairs.

Ten minutes later the stubbly old fellow appeared, still in his shirt-sleeves. 'What's the hurry?' he grumbled.

He went into his office and started to fumble about with keys and things. Six-thirty struck on the tinny clock.

'I say,' Michel called, 'our train goes in fifteen minutes.'

'Coming, coming. Here we are.' He came out of the office and threw the cards on the counter. 'All in good time, you see.'

We took the cards and hurried out into the darkness. The cold air was clean and invigorating after the foul atmosphere of this doss-house. We were pleased to see that there were a fair number of people about, and we spent the next ten minutes walking aimlessly in order to restore our circulation.

'What do you think the next step is?' I asked after we had gone some way.

'I don't think we should risk calling on our contact till after eight-thirty. He might be in bed, and that'd mean hanging about in the street. I think we ought to try and get something to eat.'

'But we haven't any bread tickets,' I reminded him.

'We'll have to try anyway. I'm famished.'

'So am I. But it might be an idea to find out how close we are to the Place Thornigy [where our contact lived] before we do anything else.'

Michel agreed and we went to look at the large map which was displayed outside the nearby Métro station. By sheer good luck we found that the Place Thornigy was quite close.

'We may as well go and have a look at the place first and then try to get something to eat.'

We stepped out briskly, trying to get warm, each of us carrying his own suitcase. We were talking so much that we omitted to keep a good look-out, and suddenly we found that we had blundered right on to a large control. A section of Germans all armed with rifles had cordoned off the area where we were about to walk. There was no going back; it would be too obvious that we were dodging. So we walked on, passing through the cordon of Germans, straight into the blocked area. We stopped for a few moments near one soldier who was busily unwrapping a parcel belonging to a workman; as he completed his search we moved on, close to two other soldiers who were questioning a man in a beret about his papers; each time we moved we edged near a German who was already fully occupied. As we neared the far side of the enclosed area we opened up our cases and then, reaching the cordon, closed them up again in a very ostentatious way, chatting about the coldness of the morning. No one paid the slightest attention to us. But without *cartes de travail* it had been a close thing. My feet felt like lead as we walked down the street.

The Place de Thornigy was a slum area. Number 26 was a lock-up garage, and there was no one about. A high wall on the other side of the road masked a grimy factory. There was a door by the side of the garage, with a bell-push let into the door-post. The two-storied house above the garage looked deserted; the windows were uncurtained and thick with dust.

'Let's go and eat,' I said.

We found a café a short distance away which was already open and went inside. A few workmen were eating croissants and sipping coffee. The place was full of steam. All they would give us was coffee; it tasted as though it was made of roasted peas. There was no milk or sugar. We poured in a small bottle of vaguely sweet liquid they gave us instead. We sat in the café till eight o'clock and then went back to the Place Thornigy. We were ravenously hungry.

At number 26 we gave the bell a long pull and waited, then we rang again. Nothing. We thumped on the door. We were about to renew the assault when a gendarme came strolling round the corner of the alley, so we moved away.

'Probably still in bed,' I muttered hopefully.

'Let's try somewhere else for food,' was all Michel could say.

We found another restaurant, a rather more expensive-looking one where, after much bargaining, we were served with croissants and something that almost tasted like real coffee. Two rolls were nothing like enough to satisfy our appetites, but they were better than nothing.

'I think I'll go back and try again on my own,' Michel said at last. 'Two of us are a bit conspicuous. You wait here.'

He returned ten minutes later, looking worried.

'Let's go,' he said.

'What's the matter?' I asked when we had got outside.

'I'll tell you. I knocked and rang several times and nothing happened. Then a woman came out from the next-door house and stared at me for a minute. She strolled towards me and as she passed she whispered, "The Gestapo raided that house a few days ago." That means the place was probably being watched and if it were—'

'You've probably been followed,' I said.

'Exactly.'

'The sooner we know the better. Let's start walking.'

We did so, and soon came to a Métro station where we ducked down the stairs and bought ourselves tickets. Our plan was to go to some fairly unfrequented area of the suburbs and there get off the train and see who followed us; the sooner we knew who our follower was – if there was one – the easier it would be to deal with him. Neither of us knew Paris well, but eventually our train came to a station which seemed quite deserted and we got out. Only three other people did so – a young woman, an old lady on bent black-stockinged legs, and a man in a raincoat and soft brown hat.

We came out of the station and found ourselves by the banks of the Seine; the grey waters swirled under the parapet. No one was about; there was no cover save for some small trees along the pavement. If we had a follower he would have to show himself or discontinue the search. We started walking slowly along the embankment.

A hundred yards further on we stopped and leaned over the parapet. When we glanced back the way we had come, the man in the raincoat and the brown hat was walking slowly along in our direction. It was clear that we must eliminate the menace before it grew greater; if the man were to able to call for help it would become very hard to get away. We crossed the road, quite slowly and obviously, and went down a side turning, then into a mews opening off it. There was no one about and we were overlooked only by two high windows. We stopped just round the corner and flattened ourselves against the wall. As soon as the man turned into the mews we planned to put him out of action. We did not expect to have much difficulty as Michel was a brawny six foot two, and in every way the complete athlete, while I, not so hefty, had had extensive training in unarmed combat. We stood and waited, but no one came; no footstep sounded in the road. We waited tense and expectant for five minutes and then relaxed, picked up our cases, walked out of the mews and back on to the embankment. A long way down the lonely pavement we saw the man in the raincoat and the brown hat, strolling homewards in a leisurely manner.

'So much for the Gestapo,' I smiled.

The temptation to go off into giggles in such situations was very strong, a natural reaction against the intense strain of fear.

'It's not quite as simple as that,' Michel reminded me. 'If the woman was right and the Gestapo did raid the Place Thornigy, it means that we can't possibly risk going back there. We're lucky the Gestapo weren't there when we called; I suppose our contact managed to hold his tongue or else put them on the wrong trail.'

'Thank God for it,' I replied. 'All the same, it means we're stuck in Paris without any idea how to get any farther.'

'I've got some friends,' Michel said. 'They live near the Quai de

Tokio. I haven't heard from them in two years, but I suppose there's a good chance that they're still there. I think I'd better go and see them right away. Probably best if I go alone in case there's any trouble.'

We walked along together to the Quai de Tokio which was not far away. Michel's friends lived in a block of modern flats facing the river. A footbridge crossed the Seine nearby, and we arranged to meet there at 1 o'clock (it was now nearly 10 a.m.).

'If I haven't turned up by one-fifteen you'd best carry on alone,' Michel said.

'Good luck,' was the only reply I could think of, and with that we parted. I crossed the bridge and started to walk in that aimless and depressing way one has when alone in a strange city. It was a long time since I had had anything like a decent meal and it was still extremely cold. The north wind cut like a scythe through the broad empty streets of the grey French capital. If Michel were to fail in his mission we were without friends of any kind, while if any ill-fortune were to befall him I would be left completely on my own without any idea how to establish contact with those who might help me. Snow began to fall heavily in fat, wet flakes.

My only object in walking was to kill time, and my only occupation to remember which way I had come so that when the time came I would be able to find my way back to where I was to meet Michel. The snow drove me to look for shelter and I found it at last under the shabby green ironwork of the overhead railway which ran along a paved boulevard. The wet snow dissolved into grey mush on the pavements and the damp penetrated my shoes. I went into a café and tried to get something to eat, but the demand for bread tickets was universal. I had a *vin blanc* as I could not face the dreadful coffee. It was quite warm in the café, but I was the only customer and the *garçon* turned out to be very inquisitive. Rather than face his questions I went out into the snow again.

As I walked along I began to think seriously about what I should do if Michel were to be caught or if he could not get in touch with his friends. Either separately or together, it seemed clear that we would have to go back to Brussels and get Victor to send a message to London asking for a new contact line. But to return to Brussels was not so easy; I had only French papers, I had no guide to take me across the frontier, and no Belgian money. In the end I decided the only thing would be to try to get as far as Tournai and there call on the lady who had led us across the frontier before. It was a bleak prospect, but at least it was something to work on. I started back towards my meeting place with Michel.

Inevitably, I arrived some ten minutes early and was forced to hang about in the slush, a strange thing to do and one that drew curious looks from the few pedestrians who passed me. The sense of loneliness was as chilling as the weather. One o'clock came. Surely it would not be long before Michel arrived? The plan to go back to Tournai, which had seemed so feasible when I did not really think I should have to use it, now seemed quite beyond me; I knew I would never be able to carry it out. One-fifteen came and went.

I should have moved off, but I could not raise the energy. My dejection was absolute; I just stood and waited like a forlorn schoolboy as the snow silted up in my collar. I turned and looked at the grey river, the snow sloping into it and disappearing without a trace. Nothing had ever looked quite so desolate.

'Thank God you're still here,' said a voice at my elbow.

I spun round. It was Michel. I grasped at his hand with both of mine and shook it, the tears pricking in my eyes.

'So you're all right?' I gasped.

'Yes, I'm all right. I'm sorry I took so long but I ran into a snap-control – at least almost ran into it – and I had to go a long way round. I was terrified you would have gone.'

'I'm frozen,' I said. 'Let's walk.' We started off. 'Now,' I said after a little, 'what's the news?'

'Well, my friends were in. They've got a small flat on the ground floor; they seemed very pleased to see me and they said they'll help us in every way they can.'

'That's wonderful,' I cried.

'There are two snags,' Michel went on. 'The first is that they've got a living-in maid and they're not at all sure about her. She goes around with German soldiers and that sort of thing. Besides, there's no spare bedroom, only a divan in the sitting-room just big enough for one.'

'Well, what's happening?'

'They say they'll put me up with them, and they're trying to find somewhere for you at the moment.'

'Well, I hope they find it soon,' I said. 'I'm just about dying from hunger.'

'Good God!' Michel exclaimed. 'I quite forgot. I've got a present for you.' He put his hand in his pocket and drew out a packet which, to my greedy eyes, looked like a sandwich. So it was, and after eating it I felt a very different person; as if to mark the change in my fortunes, the sun began to come through the banked clouds overhead.

We went into a small café to discuss the future. As in the case of the cover story in the tram at Hergnies, our minds had worked along very similar lines.

'So I think I should go back to Brussels,' was Michel's conclusion. 'I'll start just as soon as we've found you somewhere to stay.'

'That's absurd,' I protested. 'I don't see why you should.'

'There's no point in our both going,' he answered.

'No, but that's no reason—'

'Be sensible. If you go and get caught without papers it's the end for you. Whereas if I get caught I can always say I've lost my papers and give them my real name and address. At least I have a genuine identity.'

'And it's probably on the wanted list,' I pointed out.

'We'll have to take that risk.'

Michel had made up his mind to make the journey and nothing I could say would persuade him to alter his decision. He left me at 4 that afternoon to go and have tea with his friends; we agreed to meet at 6 o'clock at the Pont Motoban. The maid had that evening off, so I would be able to accompany him to the flat where his friends would tell me what they had fixed up for me. That left me two hours in which to walk the streets, but this time I did not mind so much; the weather was still cold but the snow had stopped, and there was a crispness about the day which, after my sandwich meal, was almost invigorating.

My walk took me to the Eiffel Tower and my mind went back to 1934 when I had been in Paris on a trip; I had gone to the top of the tower and seen Paris laid out before me. Now it was a German wireless station. I had been told that the lifts had been sabotaged so that when the duty crew arrived to man the station they always had to climb the stairs to the top – 2,000 of them. It took an hour to make the ascent.

Michel and I were both on time for our meeting at the Pont Motoban and he took me straight to the flat. It was a place of some elegance, and I was appalled when I caught sight of myself in a gold-framed mirror. I had not shaved for three days, my hair was saturated and hung down over my face and ears, my coat was like a seal's skin and my shoes were soaked through. I shook hands with Monsieur and Madame, both charming people; he was a banker and she a well-known barrister. They were as efficient as they were delightful, and during the afternoon they had arranged everything.

'I shall take you now to a friend who has agreed to put you up,' Madame told me. 'He is a Roman Catholic priest, the head of a large boys' school in the Rue de Grenelle. His housekeeper has gone to visit her family for five or six days. You will be able to have her room till she returns.'

'That sounds perfect,' I smiled.

'Michel, you will stay here tonight?'

'Please. I shall be leaving you tomorrow morning to go back to Brussels.'

It was agreed between us that if we heard nothing from Michel by the end of a week we were to assume that something had gone wrong; then I would have to make plans to go on alone.

'If that is all set,' Madame said, 'we will leave now. I have an appointment for dinner.'

'Goodbye, Michel,' I said. 'You know what I am thinking. Thank you for doing this.'

I held out my hand and he shook it, and I followed Madame out of the flat. We just managed to dodge a snap-control as we came out of the entrance. The sooner my papers were in order the happier I would be.

We travelled by Métro to the Rue de Bac. The Rue de Grenelle was quite close by and a few minutes later Madame led me through a double carriage gate, across a yard and into a large house set well back from the road. She took me up to the third floor and knocked at a door.

'Come in!'

We went in. Monsieur l'Abbé rose from a large desk in front of the window and came over to us. He shook each of us by the hand and told me that I was very welcome. He was a scholarly-looking man of about 45 with a high forehead beneath which intelligent dark eyes watched you through gold-rimmed spectacles. Madame handed me a small parcel (which, she said, contained my supper) and then took her leave, promising to return the next day with some bread tickets for me; this would enable me to eat my meals out.

'Now then,' said Monsieur l'Abbé, who seemed to be in a high good humour, 'about these rooms. My housekeeper lives in part of the ground floor of the house next door. Quite convenient, you see, because it is well away from the school building. There is a connecting door, however, but I think it would be better if you did not come during school hours. The fewer people who know about your existence the better.'

'I quite agree,' I said.

'Now, about meals. I'm afraid I shan't be able to feed you here, but that won't matter as soon as you've some bread tickets. Once you've got those you can order a three-course meal without trouble. I'll arrange that with the local restaurant anyway.'

'I'm looking forward to that,' I smiled.

'By the way, let me take a look at your papers, may I?' I passed them across. 'Not bad,' was the verdict. 'But, of course, you must try to get a *carte de travail* as soon as possible.'

I was very tired and Monsieur l'Abbé showed me to my room early. It was at the end of a dark corridor which contained only a store cupboard and a lavatory. The room was barely furnished, but the bed looked comfortable and the place was spotlessly clean.

'I hope you manage to sleep well,' smiled Monsieur l'Abbé as he shut the door.

There was no heating of any kind in the room and there was only one cold tap over the sink. But cold as I was, I decided that a thorough wash was essential. I started off by cleaning my shoes with my handkerchief. I hung up my coat to dry, and put my trousers under the mattress. I then set about cleaning myself; I did this piece by piece to avoid the worst consequences of undressing. Nevertheless it was a chilling exercise.

As I washed I noticed some small red lumps on my body; no sooner had I noticed them than they began to irritate maddeningly. When I was hanging up my shirt I saw a tiny black spot on it and, as I watched, it jumped. Fleas! I went through all my clothes and found four more. I snatched up my piece of soap and set about trapping them, but I only got two. It did not take much to deduce where I had picked them up: they were the natural citizens of a grubby bed in a grubby hotel near the Gare du Nord.

CHAPTER 13

In Paris

It was nearly midday before I woke. I snuggled down in the bed and dozed for a while longer. Then I realized I was famished. I got out of bed and found the packet of food which Madame had given me for my supper; I had not touched it. I climbed back into bed and draped the warm bedclothes around me.

The packet contained a large hunk of bread, a waxen lump of butter and a cardboard container. I opened this curiously and was amazed to find a boned chicken in aspic. I wolfed down all the bread and butter and half the chicken, washing the whole lot down with a glass of ice water from the tap. Can it be true that the Americans drink this from choice?

It was freezing hard outside (and probably inside too). A Citroën with a tarpaulin over it stood there, beaded with ice. At 1 o'clock I dragged myself from the bed and got dressed. A little later the Abbé came in with a full-length loaf, butter, jam and a large pot of coffee. This warmed me up and I spent the afternoon wrapped in the eiderdown trying to preserve the warmth, with little success I fear. I passed the time reading a couple of books I found in the storeroom.

At 5 o'clock Madame arrived. She brought me a plentiful supply of bread tickets for which I thanked her cordially, at the same time congratulating her on the excellence of her chicken in aspic.

'*My* chicken?' she laughed. 'I'm afraid it wasn't mine. I can hardly boil an egg. My husband's the cook in our house – and aspic is a speciality of his.'

'Well, please thank him for me.'

'I will. I shall be back tomorrow, and I'll bring a friend with me who can put you in touch with an escape line. He has a nephew who got into Spain along it quite recently.'

I was not very pleased with this latest development. It seemed that they were rather too keen to get rid of me. For my part, I refused to believe that Michel would not be back within the week. All the same, I supposed that there would be no harm in having an alternative plan if by any chance he failed to return.

I was still in bed when the Abbé and Madame returned the next morning; the man who knew about the escape line was with them.

'You must excuse me,' I told them, 'but this is the warmest place I can find.'

'Of course,' Madame said. 'We would not have disturbed you, but Gaston here has some information for you.'

'I think it can be arranged for you to be taken as far as the Spanish frontier, but before we go any further with our plans they want fifty thousand francs.'

'Fifty thousand?'

'Yes, have you got it?'

'No,' I said, 'I most certainly have not.'

Even if I had, I should have been most unwilling to hand it over.

'What do you know about these people?' I asked.

'Very little,' Gaston admitted.

'I certainly wouldn't dream of making any move until the end of the week,' I said. 'In any case, the most I could possibly afford would be thirty thousand francs.'

Actually I had about 45,000, but I did not feel bound to reveal this. Madame and Gaston soon left me and the Abbé then told me that he had visited the *patronne* of a good little restaurant in the Rue des Quatre Vents near St Sulpice.

'I told them that you had had your entire family killed in the bombing of L'Orient and the shock has been almost too much for you. You'll have a table away from the other diners and you can eat before the rush begins. I've also told them not to talk to you or ask you any questions. They'll just give you your meal and that will be that.'

'I don't know how to thank you,' I said. 'But why all the precautions about no one talking to me?'

'Your accent,' he explained. 'It's very Belgian – and we in Paris are very snobbish about accents, you know.'

Just before noon, while the boys were still at their lessons, the Abbé came and collected me and took me to the restaurant. I had spent most of the morning standing in front of my mirror trying to look numb with shock and misery. However, my feelings on entering the restaurant were hardly those I was trying to simulate; the smell of a good hot meal was almost too much to bear.

The *patronne* exchanged knowing looks with the Abbé and I was led to a table by the sympathetic lady. There she installed me with clucks of goodwill and pats of solicitude and left for the kitchen. I wondered what she would bring me to eat and my mind dwelt upon numerous succulent dishes; the reality exceeded the illusion, for I was served with an enormous portion of roast turkey. I was uncertain just how much food a bereaved and heartbroken bomb victim could safely consume; in the end my desire conquered my judgment and I ate every scrap on my plate, all the while preserving an air of desperate melancholia. I gave the good lady my bread tickets and, as I paid the bill, risked one word: *Merci.* With that I waddled sadly from the restaurant.

This routine continued each day. Monsieur l'Abbé brought me bread, which he had purchased with my tickets, cheese, jam and butter, and from these I made my supper. On the Sunday, he took me to the convent of the Sisters of Charity in the Rue de Bac where, in the chapel, Our Lady had made her miraculous appearance to the Sister Catherine. The Reverend Mother took me into the chapel and showed me the actual chair on which Our Lady was sitting at her apparition.

The Abbé told her that I was soon to make a long and dangerous journey, whereupon she gave me three small sacred medals, one for me and one for my friend.

'But what is the third one for?' I asked.

'For your wife,' she explained, 'when you reach home safely.'

I had been with the Abbé for five days when he received a postcard from his housekeeper saying that she was returning the next day.

'You must move at once,' he said.

'I'd better get in touch with Michel's friends.'

'I will telephone them,' the Abbé promised.

He returned with the news that they had told their maid that she could have the afternoon off; I was to go round and see them when she was out. I walked to the flat, greatly enjoying the exercise after being cooped up in my room for so long. They were both very good to me and I had my first cup of real tea since leaving England.

'We've found somewhere else for you,' Madame told me proudly. 'It's right on the other side of Paris though. Can you be ready to move this evening?'

'I can be ready in three minutes,' I assured them.

'I will take you there,' Monsieur said quietly. 'But I think it would be better for security if you did not actually speak to me. I shall be waiting at the entrance to the Métro in the Rue de Bac – you know it?'

'Certainly.'

'Good. At eight o'clock sharp. You'll see me all right and I'll lead the way. Buy yourself a ticket and keep an eye on me because we have to change halfway.'

'I'll be there,' I said.

I went back and told the Abbé that everything was under control and tried to thank him for all he had done.

'It was nothing,' he said, 'really. I am only sorry that you have to go. I am working late tonight, so perhaps you would call on me before you leave?'

I said I would be happy to do so and I returned to his study at about half-past seven, ready to say goodbye.

'Ah,' he said, 'you must not go without a drink. We must toast your success.'

So saying, he produced a bottle of cognac and a couple of glasses. We had several glasses before he finally let me go, and it was ten past eight before I reached the Métro in the Rue de Bac. I saw Monsieur immediately, but he was talking to someone at the top of the subway stairs. I loitered about and waited until whoever it was had shaken hands with Monsieur and made off. We went down the steps to the Métro.

The house to which Monsieur eventually led me was almost palatial; it had an ornate white façade, and broad steps of white marble swept up to an elaborate wrought-iron door. I had joined Monsieur by this time and, when we were admitted, he introduced me to my hostess.

'This is Madame Caffaret, the celebrated pianist,' he said.

I bowed and took the lady's hand.

'Do come into the lounge,' she said, smiling.

It was a beautiful room dominated by a full-size concert grand piano. We sat down and I explained to Monsieur why I had been late for our meeting.

'It wouldn't have mattered,' he said, 'but for the fact that that friend of mine came up and started talking to me. As it happened I had thought I should have a good story to tell if I were caught in a control and asked why I was coming to see Madame here. So I bought a box of chocolates which I could say was a birthday present. Well, this friend of mine saw me standing about and asked me to come and have a drink with him. When I explained that I was waiting for someone, he asked me to bring them along too. I didn't quite know what to do; I said that I couldn't. He must have noticed my embarrassment and, more important, he also noticed the box of chocolates. Well, it was his turn to be embarrassed. "I didn't realize it was that sort of meeting," he said with a knowing smile. "I quite see you can't bring *her* along." And with that he went his way. I'm glad my wife knows the truth!'

Madame Caffaret lived with her daughter and son-in-law, both of whom I met later in the evening; all three behaved with the greatest kindness towards me. The house was very luxurious, but there was very little heat. There was an electric fire in the drawing-room and I spent much of my time in there, reading and listening to Madame playing the piano. She told me that she and Yvonne Arnaud were great friends, and that when they were both children they had been regarded as prodigies. Yvonne Arnaud had given up music for the stage and had become a brilliant actress. Madame Caffaret had continued with the piano and had given concerts all over the world.

'And do you play now?' I asked her.

'Never in public,' she replied. 'I play sometimes for private concerts when money is being raised for our French prisoners-of-war.'

Michel had now been away for a week. All the time I was feeling more and more guilty that I had allowed him to subject himself to so many dangers while I remained in safety. That seventh day went desperately slowly. Now I felt that all was lost; then that Michel was on the point of calling; then that we should escape together, or again that I had better get in touch with the other escape line. I could not eat my dinner. Then, at nearly 10 o'clock the phone rang and Madame answered it. I listened keenly for what she would say. 'I understand,' was all I heard.

'Well?' I asked, as she came back into the room.

'A message for you,' she smiled, 'from the Quai de Tokio. They told me to tell you that your friend has arrived and is well.'

I grasped her hand as though she herself were my deliverer. Michel and I met the next afternoon. I have never felt so relieved as when I saw his tall figure approaching our meeting place. The weather was fine and sunny (a welcome change) and we decided to go for a long walk; he could give me his news as he went.

'How did it all go?' I enquired eagerly. 'Was it easy or not?'

'I wouldn't say easy,' was the reply. 'The first difficulty came up right away. I went to the station and asked for a ticket to Valenciennes and the booking clerk asked me for my permit. I said, "What permit?"

The clerk told me that no long-distance ticket could be issued without written permission from the *Kommandantur*.'

'What did you do?'

'I couldn't do anything. But there happened to be an old couple just behind me in the queue and apparently they had applied for two permits and had only been given one. The clerk refused to issue more than one ticket, however, so they were roughly in the same position as I was. I heard the man say that they would have to abandon their trip. It was my only chance and I took it; I went up to him and told him that I was prepared to buy his permit if he would let me have it. He looked very suspicious for a moment and then muttered, "A thousand francs." I couldn't wait. I gave him the money and he handed over the permit. The rest was plain sailing – at least as far as the frontier. The people we met at Hergnies were very helpful and managed to let me have some Belgian money, and told me how to get back into Belgium the way we came out.'

'Was the frontier post still unmanned?' I asked.

'Yes,' Michel nodded. 'I got across all right and then I had another stroke of luck. I was just going to get on the tram to Tournai when I heard some of the passengers who had just come from there saying that the controls and checks were very rigorous; they said they'd never known anything like it. Apparently there had been some sabotage there a couple of days earlier and the place was crawling with Gestapo men. If I hadn't heard about all this I should have strayed smack into the middle of it without papers of any description. I avoided Tournai, I need hardly say, and eventually reached Brussels by a roundabout route. I got hold of Victor through Castor.'

'What did he say when he saw you? He must have been pretty surprised.'

'He thought we were safely back in England! Lucien put through a message to London, but he didn't hear anything in reply for nearly a week. Then he heard that our Place Thornigy address was definitely blown.'

'We guessed that much,' I commented. 'Did he give you another?'

'Not exactly, but we're to report daily to the receptionist at the Hotel Victoria who'll give us further instructions. We're to ask if there are any letters for Julien.'

'I see.'

'By the way, you'll never guess who I saw in Brussels.'

'Well, who?'

'Jules. He's back again – to collect more money, of course. He's still been unable to get any further than Paris. He says he's fed up with the escape line and is going to try and make his own way home. I'm rather inclined to think that's the wisest thing. Anyway, I've arranged a meeting with him while we're here if we need help in finding places to stay. Jules knows plenty.'

'Is there any other news?' I asked, feeling almost homesick for Brussels and our old companions.

'They've arrested the man and woman at the dairy in the Place Albert.'

'What for? Surely they aren't tightening up on the black market after all this time?'

'They passed a lot of airmen along the escape route, you know. I suppose someone split on them.'

'How was the return journey to Paris?' I asked, after we had walked on in silence for a while.

'No trouble at all,' he said shortly.

I could not but wonder how trouble-free a trip across Occupied Europe could be when you had no papers and were wanted by the Gestapo. The way Michel treated the whole thing, it might have been a Boy Scout's game.

'What are you doing about accommodation?'

'They're letting me stay on at the flat,' Michel told me. 'I hope Madame Caffaret will be able to keep you until we can get some information about our next move.'

Unfortunately she could not; she told me that evening that she was expecting some friends to come and stay with her shortly and I would have to leave. I met Michel the next morning, hoping that he might have heard something from the receptionist at the Hotel Victoria which would make such a move unnecessary; but this was not the case and the man told him that he might as well call every three days.

Jules was back in Paris by now and we met him that evening in the Place de la Concorde. Nowadays it is almost impossible to cross that vast concourse, the traffic is so thick and so threatening; when we met Jules a single cyclist was struggling across it up towards the Champs Elysées. A German truck was parked in the middle of the square and a few pedestrians were walking down the Rue de Rivoli. Jules promised that he would try to find me somewhere to stay and he gave me an address to go to the next morning. 'I'll go and tell them you're coming,' he said.

Michel and I went to the address he had given us the next day. We were admitted by a middle-aged woman who seemed to be expecting us. She showed us into a gloomy little sitting-room, the sole occupant of which was a fat little baby boy of some eighteen months.

'Um, yes, you should be all right here, shouldn't you? In here, I mean, for the moment. Don't let the baby worry you. He's not mine. In fact, I wonder how he got here. Ah, well. You want a room, is that it?'

'Yes—'

'Mm, a room. I think we can fix something. Of course, life's very difficult just now, don't you think? Very difficult. I said so to Marie the other day. Oh, of course you don't know Marie, do you?'

'No, we—'

'I was saying to her only the other day – would you like some coffee?'

'That's very kind of—'

'What a sweet little boy! Aren't you sweet? I wonder where he came from! Arrived this morning. You sweet thing! I suppose I'd better go and telephone now.'

Out she went. Michel and I turned to each other and shrugged.

162

We could hear the woman dialling a number in the next room and soon we heard her ask to speak to Mademoiselle Marie.

'Is that you, Marie? Oh, yes, good. Yes, I wanted to telephone you for something. Now then, what? Oh, yes, I've got two more pupils for the catechism class. Would you like to see them before I send them round? Yes, I'll tell them.'

She rang off and came back to the room where we were waiting.

'You're sure you don't want any coffee? You've only to ask . . .'

'As a matter of—'

'You poor things alone with the baby! Has he been good? I'm afraid you'll have to wait for half an hour as Madame can't get here before then. But do make yourselves at home.' She glanced over at the baby. 'Isn't he sweet?' she crooned. 'One just can't refuse them, can one? Still, I do have two already and—'

The front doorbell shrilled suddenly. She went over to the window and peered through the lace curtains to see who was there. 'Oh dear, oh dear! Now this is trying, most trying. I don't really know what to do – um – I wonder what the best thing would be—'

'What's the trouble?' I demanded fiercely.

'Relations. I know! Take the baby into the other room. Quickly now. They mustn't know about you or the baby, so keep him quiet whatever you do. For goodness' sake, don't make a sound.'

She pushed us hurriedly into the next room as the front doorbell sounded again. I was left holding the baby.

We found ourselves in a small bedroom, very dark and very cold. I sat down with the baby in my arms, on the bed; it squeaked continuously. The baby sat on my knee and stared at me insolently. I stared back. This disconcerted the child, for he suddenly made a grab at my glasses.

'You little—' I cried, saving them from his grasp.

The baby gurgled contentedly. Michel and I tried to 'shush' him, but the sound we made only produced a further spate of gurgling noises. Luckily the conversation in the next room was loud enough to drown the child's cooings. I laid him gently on the bed and he lay there kicking his legs in the air and not making a sound. After twenty minutes we heard the visitors leave. The bedroom door soon opened and the woman reappeared.

'My goodness me!' she exclaimed, wiping her brow. 'They were my two sisters and a brother-in-law. They're all terribly pro-German. I just don't know what would have happened if they'd found you here. I don't know what I would have said – I just can't think.'

'Well,' I said, as soothingly as I could, 'it doesn't really matter now, does it?'

The doorbell rang again.

'If they've come back,' said the woman as she went to answer it, 'I don't know what I shall say. If they find you here, I simply . . .'

But this time it was the woman who had come to see us. She introduced herself as Comtesse d'Harcourt and we found her a little more reliable than our hostess. She was glad that we only needed one room and said that she could manage that easily, though it meant sleeping in the servants' quarters.

'I don't think that will matter greatly,' I assured her.

'In that case, here is the address of my flat. Perhaps you would come at six o'clock this evening?'

'I will be there,' I said. 'And thank you very much.'

We said goodbye to the baby and our hostess showed us to the door.

'You know,' she told us as we left, 'if they'd found you I don't know what I would have said . . .'

'Well,' I observed when we were clear of the house, 'I'm glad that's over. It's one of the most irritating mornings I've ever spent. And by the way, while on the subject of irritations, have you suffered from fleas at all?'

'So you've got them too!' Michel exclaimed. 'I have been scratching myself for the past week. And I still haven't got rid of the last of them, even after several hot baths.'

The Comtesse and her husband turned out to be excellent hosts and their flat was the first place I had stayed in where I did not shiver incessantly. They were wealthy people, and were able to burn wood from their estate in the country. I spent two weeks with them, as it turned out, and thoroughly enjoyed the time; we fed very well, and since the Comtesse had been a Mademoiselle Clicquot we were not without liquid assets. Only one meal was spoiled for me and that was when, on helping myself to vegetables, I noticed a small black spot on my wrist – one of those damned fleas again. Even as I saw it, it jumped, heading straight for the Comtesse; I only hope it never reached her or, if it did, that she did not divine its source.

I saw Michel every few days but it was two weeks before there was a message for him at the Hotel Victoria. It was merely that we were to walk up a certain road in Paris at exactly 11.30 the next morning.

'That's rather vague, isn't it?' I said, when he told me.

'That's all there was, so we'll have to do as we're told.'

We met at exactly the time we had been instructed, and began to walk slowly up the street; it was quite short and seemed deserted. We had no notion of what was supposed to happen and felt not so much apprehensive as curious. As we started to walk a woman came out of a house ahead of us carrying a large shopping basket. She stared at us closely. We increased our pace and disappeared round a corner, returning a few minutes later when we might reasonably have expected her to be gone. We turned the corner and found that the road was indeed empty again, and once more we started to walk down it. To our astonishment the same woman came out from the same house.

'She must have forgotten something, I suppose,' Michel said.

I shrugged and we walked on past her again.

'Here – you!' she called out. 'Aren't you the two blokes I'm supposed to be meeting here at eleven-thirty?'

I do not know why, but we had both been expecting a man. Slightly taken aback, we turned round and went back to her.

'We were expecting to meet someone here at eleven-thirty,' agreed Michel.

'*Eh bien*,' she said and, opening her handbag, produced three photographs. 'Can you name these three people?'

I immediately recognized Ping-Pong, whose reception in Belgium I have already described, while the other two were agents whom I had known in England during training. Their code names were Grandpère and Greyhound; I told her so.

'That is fine,' she commented. 'You must be Hillcat and this is your friend from Brussels.'

'Quite right.'

'Let's all go and have a drink, shall we? Afterwards we shall get some lunch. I hope you have plenty of money with you because I am taking you to a place where the food is excellent and the price incredible. Louis has booked a table for twelve o'clock, so we shall just be in time. Come.'

Louis turned out to be the owner of a restaurant just near the Etoile; the food was as magnificent as our guide had forecast, and as we ate Louis inspected our papers. Luckily there was no one else in the restaurant, for his comments were many and loud.

'Look at this, I ask you,' he bellowed. 'These numbers are in the wrong place – and the photographs too! Here, Fernand, come and look at this.' The waiter came over and peered over Louis' shoulder. 'Just look at that rubber stamp . . . Would that take you in for a moment? Of course it wouldn't. Not a chance. And they haven't got any *cartes de travail* at all! Still, we can soon fix that. Have you got any spare photographs?'

Luckily we had, and handed them over.

'Well, we'll try to have something ready for you by Friday. Meanwhile I suppose you'd better have these back – for what they're worth.'

'That means we can leave Paris on Friday night,' Madame said. 'We shall take the night train to Toulouse. I can bring your papers with me to the station; I'll see you on the platform at eight-thirty.'

'Where should we book to?' Michel enquired.

'Right through to Pau. You'll be catching the connection at Toulouse. I'll put you in touch with another contact there who can look after you on the next stage of your trip. By the way, we'll split up when we get on the train, so that if one's caught the others still have a chance.'

'Of course,' Michel agreed. 'Are there any particular snags we're likely to run into on the way?'

'The main danger is at Vizeron – that used to be the demarcation point between Occupied and Vichy France – there'll probably be a pretty thorough check there. We arrive there about midnight.'

'It's a devil of a long trip, isn't it?' I commented. 'I suppose there's no chance of getting a Lysander to pick us up, is there?'

'There are four people waiting already,' she replied, 'and they've been waiting over three months. You can only do these operations for about six days in each moon period, and in the winter the weather makes even those pretty dangerous. Besides, we're very short of suitable fields as well.'

Apparently the first man on the list was an agent who had been dropped into France well over a year before. He had suffered a compound fracture of his left leg on landing owing to the fact that his parachute did not open properly. His wireless operator had landed safely, but had had to leave him where he was; the organization allowed him no alternative. All he could do was to go and knock up the local farmer and explain what had happened, begging him to help his friend. The farmer was a patriot who went out at once with a wheelbarrow and brought the man back to his farm. So severe were the agent's injuries, however, that he could do nothing for him; accordingly he phoned the local hospital and told them that he had found a badly injured man by the side of the road who said he had been knocked down by a German army lorry. The hospital accepted the story and the patient had to have his left leg amputated at the thigh. He was in hospital for nearly six months, which gives some indication of the seriousness of his injuries; yet, on his release, he immediately contacted his organization and did much valuable work for them.

He was now due to return home and of course the only way for him to do so was by plane. Grandpère was to accompany him and they had been waiting in the country near a suitable field during the last two moon periods. One attempt to pick them up had been made two weeks earlier, but the plane had been shot down on the way. They were still waiting. Actually, the operation was successfully carried out in March, but that was after we had left Paris.

That evening I found in my pocket a notice of a charity concert which Madame Caffaret had given me while I was still staying with her. I must have put it there and forgotten about it. Now I saw that there was an address on it to which donations could be sent and decided to do so. I slipped a 1,000-franc note into an envelope and enclosed a piece of paper on which I wrote 'With Mr Churchill's Compliments'; after all I could scarcely claim the donation as my own, seeing that it was the Government's money!

On Friday evening Michel called for me at the flat. I said goodbye to the Comtesse and the Comte and they said they would listen eagerly to the B.B.C. in order to hear the news that we had arrived safely (I had told them what message would be on the *Messages Personnels*) and that they would open a bottle of Clicquot to celebrate it.

We travelled to the Gare du Midi by Métro. After Michel's experience, I was rather worried about how easily we would be able to buy tickets all the way to Pau. In the event there was no difficulty and we proceeded to the platform; Madame and Louis were waiting for us by the barrier.

'I thought I'd come and see you off myself,' Louis told us. 'Besides, I just had to come and give you your new papers in person; they are so beautiful.'

However beautiful they were we could not see to admire them, so strict was the blackout. After Louis had shaken us all by the hand seven or eight times, we split up and got on the train at intervals of two to three minutes. Michel and I found seats in the same compartment and Madame was a little way down the same carriage. The train left punctually at 8.30 and we settled back in our seats.

Just before midnight we pulled into Vizeron. Michel and I were pretending to be asleep, but in fact both of us were listening keenly for the sound of a check being made. My apprehension was immeasurably increased by the fact that I had not found any pretext for looking at my papers, and as a result I had no idea what my name was supposed to be, where I lived or what my occupation was. A compartment door was slid open further down the carriage; then it banged shut and another one opened. We were for it. At length our own door was slid officiously open. I shifted as if in a deep sleep.

'Tickets, please!' came the cry.

The ticket collector looked as tired as I was pretending to be; he had no interest whatever in our papers. But the train did not pull out of the station; we simply stood at the platform. Every moment we expected the check to begin. It did not do so, however, and twenty minutes later, we moved off. It was our lucky night.

We arrived in Toulouse at 8 o'clock in the morning. With an hour to wait before catching the train to Pau, we decided to try to get some breakfast at the station buffet. All they had was broth; there was nothing at all to eat. We left the buffet and went back on to the platform; we found a quiet spot and there we inspected our papers in order to discover who we were supposed to be. I found I was a Monsieur Le Grand and lived in the Rue Pigalle in Paris; I was married, but had no children. My *carte de travail* showed that I was a commercial traveller working for a firm of stove-makers: the second time I had been pushed into the stove business! Unfortunately the rubber stamp of the firm had been so badly smudged that I could read neither their name nor the address.

'Can you make it out all right?' I asked Michel.

'Only too well. I'm five years younger on my *carte de travail* than I am on my identity card!'

'Let me see. Heavens above!' I cried as soon as I saw Michel's papers.

'Something else wrong?' he asked.

'Look,' I said, showing my papers to him, 'they're all written in the same handwriting and with the same ink. But they're supposed to have been issued in different places by different people.'

'So much for Louis and his high standards of forgery!'

'If I could get hold of him . . .' I muttered vindictively.

'Well, it's too late now. We'd better put these away and hope for the best. I won't give much for our chances if there's a stiff check.'

The passengers for Pau were now crowding on to the platform and getting on the train. We saw Madame get on and thought it was time we did so ourselves. Again we managed to find seats in the same compartment and, since we had had no breakfast, took the precaution of booking two places for the 11.30 lunch for which the steward was canvassing with a little bell.

Our journey took us through lovely country and we began to enjoy it; our enjoyment led to lunchtime coming all the sooner and we made our way along the corridors of the swaying train to the restaurant car. Again we pretended to be strangers but still contrived to sit at the same table and get into conversation. We shared it with two other travellers and we were all talking and eating the surprisingly good food being served when the door at the end of the car opened. A civilian and two Germans in uniform came in.

'All papers ready, please,' said the civilian in a polite voice. My easy good humour vanished; every muscle contracted. I looked at Michel, who was pale and tense. We knew how poor our papers were. It was a matter of waiting; we tried to go on eating. The men in uniform appeared to be responsible for military personnel only, while the civilian attended to the remainder who, of course, greatly outnumbered them. The latter seemed very busy and my hopes rose as I saw how quickly he moved from table to table; he was looking only at identity cards, checking that the photographs tallied with the bearers and then returning them to their owners with a polite thank you. 'Thank you,' I heard him say. 'Thank you. Thank you.' Now he was coming towards us. Our table was at the end of the carriage and the two soldiers – who had concluded their check before their colleague – stood and waited by it. I could feel the sweat trickling down my collar. If only he would come quickly and get it over – if only he would not come yet – if only . . .

'Your papers, please.'

170

The two others at our table passed their cards across at once. Michel and I took out our wallets. The man examining the other two cards glanced for a second at the owners and then handed them back.

'Thank you. Thank you.'

He took Michel's card from him and looked at it quickly. He half stretched out his hand to return it, then he stopped and looked at the card more carefully. He turned it over; he looked up at Michel and said, 'Where are you going, please?'

'To Pau,' Michel replied in a miraculously level voice.

'I see. Would you be kind enough to show me your *carte de travail?*'

The landscape fled past the window. The other diners had returned to their food. Michel took out his wallet again and handed over his *carte*.

My heart was thumping so rapidly that I was literally surprised that no one else could hear it. My hand was shaking so much that I thrust it into my pocket; it met something small and hard, three things to be exact – the medals which the Mother Superior had given me in the convent in the Rue de Bac. The Gestapo man was holding Michel's two cards side by side. How could he miss the discrepancy in the dates of birth and the fact that they were in the same writing? I sat there waiting for the fatal words, so politely spoken, 'Would you please accompany me?' When he saw that my papers were in the same writing, my fate would be no different.

I closed my eyes as if to escape, knowing that this was the end, my hand tightly gripping the three medals in my pocket; all I could think was, 'It's up to you – it's up to you.' The longer he took, the more certain became our arrest. And still he was standing there with the two cards in his hand. But what was he doing now? He was leaning forward across the table with the papers held out to Michel.

'Thank you,' he said, picking up my card which lay on the table. He scarcely glanced at it. 'Thank you,' he said again as he returned it.

Our two dining companions, unaware (but how could they be?) that anything unusual had happened, had finished their lunch and soon returned to their seats. Michel and I looked at each other. He was white and drawn. We managed a feeble smile, not daring to speak. My hand was still in my pocket and now I drew it out, one of the medals between my fingers. I held it out to Michel.

'She did it,' I whispered.

CHAPTER 14

Travelling South

We stood in the corridor most of the rest of the way to Pau, discussing what we had at last come to believe was true – our miraculous escape. It was astonishing that after all the suspicion which he had evidently felt, the Gestapo man should have allowed us to evade him. Michel's papers had obviously struck him as peculiar and one could not believe that, on closer inspection, he had not noticed the inconsistencies of which we were so painfully conscious. For a while we thought that they were going to trap us later, perhaps hoping that we would lead them to those who were helping us, but this unhappy theory was exploded when we saw the Gestapo man and his two henchmen get off the train at Tarbes.

We steamed into Pau in the middle of the afternoon, left the station and took the short funicular up to the esplanade. So engrossed had we been in our conversation that we had not been paying much attention to the landscape, but now its magnificence could not but command all one's interest. I was struck speechless in the middle of a sentence; in the clear fresh air the mountains stood sentry, peak upon peak, against the sky. The setting sun tinged them with rosy light, while the smooth flanks of the foothills were overshadowed by the great range behind and so took on a delicate grey hue which shaded into black as the sun disappeared.

'Ah, here you are,' called a voice at our elbow. 'I've been looking for you. Is everything all right?'

'We were just admiring the view.'

'Yes? Well, you'll catch your death of cold in this wind if you stand here much longer. Come on, we'll get along to the hotel.'

This stood in a small side street and Madame was evidently well known for the *patronne* greeted her by her Christian name and asked, laughing, whether she had brought more 'travellers' with her. Madame introduced us and we filled in the necessary forms.

'I suppose you'll want our identity cards for the Gestapo,' Michel said, remembering our experience in Paris.

'Oh, no, they will not be required; the Gestapo look only at the register.'

'You won't be able to eat here, by the way,' Madame told us, 'but we will arrange for you to do so at the little restaurant next door.'

'Another thing,' interrupted the *patronne*, 'if anyone asks you why you are here you can tell them that you have come to see the fights.'

'Fights?'

'There are some important boxing matches arranged for next week. Many people are here to see them.'

'Is there any news of François?' Madame asked our hostess.

'I saw him the day before yesterday and he said he was going off for a week's fishing. He said he wouldn't be back till today week.'

'That means another wait, I'm afraid,' Madame told us. 'And I'm sorry, but I can't stay with you; I have some urgent work to attend to in Limoges next week. I shall stay until Sunday, but then I shall have to leave you to await François' return.'

There was no place where I should have preferred to endure the ensuing delay; even though it was wartime, there was a festal air about the town of Pau and even the blackout was not strictly observed. Michel and I visited the famous castle of Henri IV and saw his exquisite and (I should think) extremely uncomfortable bed; we went to a boxing match and frequented the cinemas, but my own favourite pastime was standing on the esplanade watching the play of shadows on the great Pyrenees.

We soon got to know the names of the various peaks, many of them in Spain. How we wished we were there too! On clear days it looked as though we could arrive in a couple of hours' brisk walking – until we realized that we should have to scale some of those peaks to get there. While we enjoyed our actual stay we could not look forward to crossing the frontier with much eagerness, particularly when sitting in the cafés we would find ourselves next to a group of German border guards at whose feet lay their huge, alert Alsatian dogs. They were friendly enough in the cafés, but I imagined their reaction to us would be the reverse of welcoming if they were to come across us nearer the frontier.

Michel and I bought ourselves Basque berets, so that we might tone better with the neighbourhood; actually, the real Basque berets are red, but we compromised with the more discreet blue. François, our next contact, turned up at breakfast time on Sunday.

'I am most frightfully sorry, you understand,' he said, 'but the message telling me to expect you did not arrive till after I had left. It was there when I returned. You must forgive me. At any rate, we can now go ahead at once. We shall be catching the four o'clock train. Book single tickets as far as Mauleon. I will be at the station to meet you.'

'Is there any good excuse we can make for going to Mauleon?' Michel asked. 'Surely it is very close to the frontier area?'

'You are right; it is,' said François. 'Luckily, however, they are holding an exhibition of modern paintings there which has attracted a number of important critics. Perhaps you might be interested in buying some of these masterpieces?'

At 3.45 we met François at the station.

'There is one change we have to make on the way,' he told us. 'And there'll be a half-hour wait, otherwise it's quite straightforward.'

Michel and I looked at our fellow passengers with some misgivings on the train; though we had got as far as berets we looked very different from the rugged, deeply bronzed, Basque folk who accompanied us. So different were we, in fact, that we decided to abandon the pretence of travelling separately; two well-dressed strangers on the same local train would be a rather unlikely event. We would attract less suspicion if we stayed together.

While in Pau we had tried to get Michel a new set of papers in which the dates of birth tallied; unfortunately, this had proved impossible and so we had resorted to changing the date on the *carte de travail* and placing beside the alteration a formidable set of initials. We had had to buy four bottles of ink before we could find a match for the one on the card. Our effort was worthwhile, however; we had not gone far before the Gestapo boarded the train at a small wayside station.

'Your papers, please,' demanded the same icily polite voice.

'Where are you going?'

'To Mauleon,' I said.

'Why?'

'We were staying in Pau and heard that there was a very good exhibition of paintings there. We thought we would run down and take a look.'

'You are interested in painting?'

'In making one or two purchases,' Michel said.

'Thank you,' the man said, handing back our papers.

It had been a rather uncomfortable few minutes, but our explanation was more plausible than it might seem; many people, fearing that the franc would become valueless after the War, were buying up anything which they thought would retain its value; jewellery and paintings were favourite choices.

It was dusk when we reached the station where we had to change and by now the thermometer must have stood at well below zero. The sunshine of the days afforded some warmth, but when night came the temperature dropped sharply. As Michel and I tramped up and down the platform to keep warm, Francois sat on a luggage trolley and dozed off; he seemed quite unaffected by the cold.

'I say, if we walk a bit closer to that train on the siding there we might find some shelter,' I suggested.

A long train consisting of completely enclosed goods trucks was standing in the siding; snow had blown in under its wheels and it had clearly been there some days.

'This is better,' I commented as we walked under the shelter of the train.

'It's certainly a bit warmer,' Michel said, 'but I don't much care for the smell.' Indeed, a most noisome smell emanated from the trucks.

Suddenly I stopped short in my tracks. There was a small aperture about a foot square, covered with thick wire-netting, set in the middle of each truck about four feet from the ground. I had glanced idly through one, and what I saw had been responsible for my sudden halt. The dead white, staring face of a man was pressed against the netting; black hair fell across it and it was framed in a jet beard; the eyes were dark pits. As I watched, another face took the place of the one I had first seen; it presented the same grim aspect. I went up to the truck and whispered through the netting, 'Who are you?' There was no reply; a few seconds later a third face took the place of the one I had spoken to. We walked the length of the train; at each aperture one of those tragic faces was pressed. No sound came from any of the trucks.

I felt as though I would pass out, I was so deeply shocked and horrified by the impression I received. Michel and I hurried back to tell François what we had seen. He knew all about it.

'It's a trainload of Russian prisoners,' he told us. 'I managed to get a few words with one of them who spoke a little French. They've been in that train for over ten days – he hadn't any idea how much over ten days, because they've lost all count of time. There are fifty of them in each of those trucks—'

'It's not possible,' I said.

'It's true. They have to take it in turns to get a little fresh air. One minute each they take, and then they have to wait an hour till their next turn. They hadn't the faintest notion where they were. I told them it was the South of France and they were astonished. They travel mostly by night – but they've been in that siding for over three days now and they don't know when they'll move again.'

'Do they get anything to eat or drink?' I asked.

'Once a day the Boches give them something, heaven knows what, but they're never allowed to leave the trucks – not for any reason.'

'It's unspeakable,' Michel muttered. 'It's not possible.'

'It's true,' said François. 'The conditions in there can't be very pretty, can they? Besides, the trucks aren't big enough for more than ten of them to get any sleep at the same time—'

'You mean they have to sleep in their own filth?'

'Of course they do. You don't think that smell is kitchen slops, do you?'

We were not sorry when our train came in and we were able to get away from the obsessive atmosphere of bitter and unrelievable suffering. That there was nothing we could do for them was like a knife in one's very soul; I shall never forget the white faces and the dark caverns that were eyes and that stared and stared, hopeless, through the crisscross of the black netting. And the silence – the silence was the silence of living death.

Mauleon was in darkness when we arrived. François led us through the barrier and there we found our next contact waiting for us. François introduced him as L'Allemand. Before we could thank François for his help he had disappeared into the gloom.

'Follow me, please,' said L'Allemand.

He led us across a large square, and soon we came to the door of a small house where L'Allemand knocked and went in. He took us through a low doorway and we found ourselves in a broad kitchen which served as a living room as well. A family of four were in residence: an elderly man, his wife and their two adult daughters. A log fire blazed in the big open fireplace and the room was filled with the spiced aroma of burning pine.

'Well, here we are,' L'Allemand said. 'Excuse my silence on the way here, but I thought we could wait to talk. You are very welcome here, in any case, and now –' he smiled '– if you will give me your names I will introduce you to the family.'

As soon as these formalities were completed, Madame and her

daughters began to lay the table and prepare the supper. We discussed the future with L'Allemand. He seemed a person one could rely on and at the moment, in his thick lumber jacket, his breeches, his thick woollen socks and his heavy, studded leather boots, he looked as if he were ready to lead us across the mountains at a minute's notice.

'As a matter of fact,' he told us, 'we should try to get across as soon as we can; conditions in the mountains are pretty good just at present. There's been no snow for a while and the surface is hard. There are a lot more patrols about now, and the more we can keep away from the usual passes the better. I'm afraid that means the going will be hard, and you'll have some very steep and long climbs. Can you do it?'

'We shall have to,' Michel said.

'I shall be coming with you all the way to Spain,' continued L'Allemand, 'because I want to get to know the route. In future I shall be able to take people across on my own.'

'Oh, we shall have another guide then?' I asked.

'Two. The first one we pick up just a few miles away; he'll lead us over the first range and down into the next valley. There the second guide'll take over, and he'll see us the rest of the way.'

The whole thing sounded very simple, but the details which L'Allemand went on to describe made it clear that we were in for the hardest and most demanding stage of our journey.

'There's more snow on the way,' L'Allemand told us. 'Once we get started on the second stage of the trip we shall have to keep moving whatever happens. It'll mean about twelve hours' solid going. We must reach Spain before the snow comes. Anyway, the quicker you get out of Mauleon the better; there are a lot of snap-controls here – owing to our being so near the frontier, you know. Apart from that, you can't stay here for longer than three nights as we're expecting some more people. I shall see the first guide tonight and, with any luck, we should be able to set out tomorrow afternoon. I'll call in the morning and let you know the details.'

The meal which Madame served to us was excellent. While enjoying it, I thought that its excellence must have turned my head: there was a lovely old grandfather clock standing in one corner of the room and as I was eating, it seemed to me that it twice struck the same hour, once at five minute's to and once on the hour. I remakred on this and they told me that it was customary in the Basque country for all chiming clocks to strike twice; the first strike warning that it would be such-and-such an hour in five minutes' time.

L'Allemand left the house after the meal to keep his appointment with the guide. As he went out he sniffed the air and muttered, 'I don't like the look of things.'

We were tired and went to bed early. Our room was on the first floor and contained only a single bed, a washstand and a large cupboard. The one window was very small and high and I could only just see over the sill, though Michel was a bit better off.

'Well, at least there are plenty of blankets,' I noted. 'It must be about twenty below, I should think.'

'What's it matter?' Michel said. 'In two days' time we shall be in Spain.'

'Roll on the day!'

It was already light when I woke the next morning. I lay dozing in the narrow bed; the mornings being the only time when one was really warm. Slowly it began to dawn on me that it was much lighter in the room than the narrow window warranted. The whitewashed ceiling seemed to be reflecting a very white light . . .

I jumped out of bed, dashed to the window, pulled myself up on the sill and looked out. The worst had happened. The entire landscape was covered with a thick eiderdown of snow. A low wall ran across the garden and from the drifted snow against it I could gauge that about ten inches had already fallen; and it was still coming down, great flakes as big as swan's feathers dropping past the window. If only François had got us here quicker, if only he had not gone fishing, if only . . .

'We've had it,' I told Michel.

'Looks like it,' he agreed.

'It's damn certain.'

'We're still alive,' he smiled wearily, 'that's something, you know. Remember the gentleman in the restaurant car?'

L'Allemand came in while we were breakfasting.

'I'm afraid that settles us for a while,' was his comment. 'There's about a foot of snow down here and that means drifts 5–6 feet thick in the mountains.'

'What can we do?'

'We can't do anything – except wait.'

'Wait how long?' I asked.

'Either till the snow has melted considerably, which means six or seven weeks, or till it's frozen hard on top so that it'll support a man's weight. That will take at least a week – if we have the right weather. What we want is clear skies and plenty of sun during the day and hard frosts at night; that should give us a good top layer of ice – if it happens.'

'How likely is it?'

L'Allemand shrugged. Our next worry is where you can stay while we wait. You can't stop here for more than two more nights, I'm afraid. Still, don't worry; I'll make some enquiries today and let you know tonight.'

'Do you think it would be safe for us to go out for a walk?' Michel asked.

'For the next couple of days it should be. The railway is probably blocked and the Gestapo don't much like the cold.'

That morning we visited the exhibition of paintings, thinking that this would give body to our cover story if it were closely examined. We peered intently at the canvases and we demanded the price of several of them. We made notes in the margins of our catalogues and altogether presented a most studious appearance. It stopped snowing at 10 o'clock and an hour later the clouds broke up and the sun shone; soon the sky was completely blue.

We went for a long walk during the afternoon and came back ravenously hungry, a hunger which Madame soon assuaged with another excellent meal. L'Allemand did not come in till after supper.

'I've arranged for you to stay in a farm for about a week. It's a few miles out of the village, but I think that's quite a good thing. No one's likely to disturb you there. I'll call for you tomorrow afternoon. I'll get hold of a couple of bikes if I can; they'll make the trip a lot easier.'

We did not sleep so well that night; Michel developed a cough and it kept both of us awake. By morning he was feeling really rotten; he decided to stay in bed till lunchtime, but by then he was much worse. He was very flushed and even he was forced to confess that he thought he had a temperature; his throat was very sore and there was no doubt about it: he had flu. I went and explained the position to the family.

'I wonder if, under the circumstances, we could possibly stay on here?' I pleaded.

'I am most terribly sorry,' said Madame, 'but it is simply not possible. If I could help, you know I would, but—'

L'Allemand came in a few minutes later and I told him what had happened.

'One thing after another,' he said. 'And this is the worst of the lot in a way. I can't think of anyone who could take him. I suppose he can't get to the farm?'

'Quite impossible,' I said firmly.

'I don't know, I just don't know.'

'There must be somewhere he can stay,' I persisted.

'The only place I can think of is the hotel,' L'Allemand said. 'We might be able to book him in there.'

'Couldn't I stay there too?' I asked.

'No, you must go to the farm, as I said.'

He seemed very insistent, and he was risking enough for us to want to respect his wishes. We were fortunate at the hotel: Michel was given a room without any trouble and we saw him safely in bed before we left. The *patron* promised to look after him and to send for a doctor if he got any worse.

L'Allemand and I set off for the farm. Most of the snow had melted down the valley and our trip was not too bad as long as we were able to stay on the road, but for the last three miles or so we were forced to take a rough track. The snow and slush was very thick in places and the tyres of the bikes could not keep a grip on the surface; we had to dismount several times and push through the worst of it. There was no human habitation of any kind during the last part of the journey; it was wild country and swollen torrents swirled across our path, while great rocks rose on either side decked with slabs of unmelted snow. As we topped a small but thickly wooded hill we saw the farm below us. It consisted of one large stone house with a square courtyard in front of it formed of barns and outbuildings.

'Here we are,' L'Allemand said, ringing the bell loudly.

A woman of about thirty came out of the farmhouse to meet us. She and L'Allemand started to talk in Basque and I could not understand a word they were saying. They seemed to be arguing, but I could not be sure. Eventually, we all went into the house and were taken into a very large room with a rough stone floor. A huge fireplace almost filled one of the short walls; a log fire burned in it, over which there hung a big-bellied iron pot. In the centre of the room was a long, rough-cut wooden table; benches ran along either side of it. In a seat right inside the fireplace a very old man was sitting, the traditional Basque beret on his head.

'That's Grandpa,' L'Allemand explained. 'He's practically a hundred years old. Both his children are dead, but there are nine grandchildren. The woman I was talking to is the oldest of them. I'm afraid none of them speak much French – except Grandpa, and he's a bit senile. You'll have to stay here till I come and fetch you.'

'How long will that be?' I asked apprehensively.

'About a week or ten days – if the weather holds. The family are a little nervous of having you here, so will you stay indoors? The odd local farmer is likely to drop over and they don't want anyone to see you.'

'Do all the family live here?'

'Seven of them, and there are two hired men as well.'

'Well, there we are,' I said gloomily.

'Cheer up,' grinned L'Allemand, holding out his hand. 'It won't be long.'

With that he left me. The eldest granddaughter was anything but pleased to see me; she went about her task of preparing a meal, all the while regarding me with the greatest suspicion. I sat down by the fire near the old man and had a look round the place. There was a large door in one of the walls and I guessed that this led straight into a cowshed; judging from the ringing of cowbells and the clanking of pails, it was milking time.

Grandpa seemed to be asleep. He was hunched forward, leaning on his stick, his head cupped in his hands. Innumerable cats played about around his feet; I do not know whether it was a cat or an involuntary moment of the old man's, but suddenly the stick slipped and he pitched forward. Had it not been for my prompt assistance he would have fallen into the fire. The woman helped me to pick him up and favoured me with the first glimmer of a smile I had had since my arrival.

'He is always falling into the fire,' she explained in very bad French.

The incident had awoken the old man, who opened his eyes and said, 'When is food going to be ready?' There was no reply. 'I always have to wait for my food. I'm the only person in the world who has to sit around all day, waiting for people . . .'

He grumbled on without the woman paying the slightest attention. Then suddenly he caught sight of me. 'Don't you agree that it's disgraceful,' he demanded, 'that I always have to wait for my dinner? What is that woman doing?'

I nodded nervously; I was so unwelcome that I felt I should agree with whoever was speaking. The old man rambled on, talking a strange language compounded of Basque and French. He continually asked questions but never expected you to answer them; probably he was too deaf to hear whether you had done so or not.

At 6 o'clock the two youngest children returned from school. They stopped dead when they saw me and for the next ten minutes neither of them said a word; they simply stood and stared with curiously intent expressions. Eventually they sat down and the woman gave them some sewing to do, but even then they continued to be fascinated by me and kept looking up as if to make sure that I was really there; I smiled at them, but at once they averted their eyes and went back to their sewing. However, the curiosity of the children was nothing to that of the adults when they returned from their work in the fields. They stood round in a semi-circle and stared at me for minutes on end; none of them said a word.

'Good evening,' I stammered after a while.

They all nodded, unsmiling, but no one spoke. Their vigil was broken only by the eldest granddaughter calling them to supper. This consisted of stew which had been cooking in the big pot over the fire; tin plates and spoons were handed out and we all queued up by the fireplace to receive our proper portion. We then went and sat at the table where a huge loaf of bread was passed around; each of us broke off a large hunk and set about our stew. Grandpa did not stir from his place by the fire and his granddaughter served him there. Still no one spoke, but the place was far from silent; the variety of noises which the assembled company made while devouring their food was startlingly uninhibited. The food at length loosened their tongues and conversation became general, my presence being forgotten or ignored.

After the meal we all washed up our plates and Grandpa was put to bed on the couch; this last manoeuvre made me slightly uneasy, for it was clear that he must have the best and most comfortable bed, yet the couch where he was now sleeping was not of a very modern or well-sprung variety. About 8 o'clock the company stood up; it was bedtime. There was no sanitation of any kind: you simply went out into the darkened yard and found yourself a likely-looking wall.

When I returned, the oil lamps were doused and one of the men led the way up the ladder into the loft. It was not easy to see the plan on which space was apportioned; as far as I could see the loft was divided in two halves and the men slept on one side and the women on the other. The floor was covered with thick straw and there was a large heap of grey blankets in one corner. As you came up the ladder into the loft you collected your blankets and found yourself a patch of floor. The men simply took off their boots and coats, loosened their belts, wrapped themselves in their blankets and lay down. I did the same, not without some misgivings. Actually, I was not uncomfortable and found that I kept very warm.

By a special dispensation I was allowed to stay in bed till 6.30 the next morning; the others were up by 5 a.m. and I could hear them as they milked the cows and led them out to pasture. When I went downstairs I was given a small enamel dish containing a little warm water.

'For the shaving and the washing,' explained the eldest granddaughter in her appalling French.

'I should be very grateful if I might have a little more hot water,' I said after I had used the small amount in the dish.

This request was ignored and so, for most of the time, was I. I was not allowed to go out and I had no books to occupy me; the days seemed endless. Their pattern never varied; breakfast at 6.30, lunch (stew) at 12 and supper (stew) at 7. The hours between I spent sitting, just sitting, and stopping Grandpa from falling into the fire. I was almost grateful when he threatened to do so, since it was the only relief I had from the utter tedium of the place. The days seemed to stretch out as my sojourn grew longer. The only good thing was that the weather stayed exactly as we wanted it; it froze hard at night and thawed slightly, under a bright sun, during the day.

By the fifth day I was feeling almost crazy with boredom. I had run out of cigarettes and I was anxious about Michel. I found innumerable things to worry about. I spent most of the day pacing up and down the dingy room. I offered to sweep the room; I begged to be allowed to peel some potatoes; I asked for a piece of rag with which to clean the windows. Anything was better than just sitting. At about 5 o'clock the monotony was disturbed by the excited entry of the eldest granddaughter.

'You will have to leave,' she told me. 'I have just heard from a neighbour that the Gestapo are in the district. They are looking for you.'

After the first flare of panic I calmed down. I was almost grateful that some pretext for my leaving the place was now available.

'Please, you must go. The Gestapo—'

'I can't possibly go now,' I said brusquely. 'It's getting dark already and I should never be able to find my way back to Mauleon. Even in daytime I don't suppose I should be able to. Still, I'll go first thing in the morning.'

'You must go now. We cannot allow you to stay here any longer. We have risked enough already—'

'I'm staying,' I said.

She left me abruptly and I could hear her talking to her brothers in the yard outside. Soon she returned.

'You must pack up all your things and take them into one of the barns. You can hide there.'

'All right.'

'But if the Gestapo find you, you must swear that you will say you sneaked into the barn for shelter and that you do not know any of us here. If you don't, it won't make any difference because we shall all swear that we do not know you.'

'Fair enough,' I agreed.

'Thank you,' she said, trying to smile. 'If you do this thing for us, tomorrow I will guide you to Mauleon. I have things to do there anyway, and I will be cycling.'

'That will be perfect,' I told her.

I was comparatively unalarmed about the Gestapo scare, being pretty sure in my own mind that it was merely a device to get rid of me.

The barn where I had to spend the night was pitch dark, but I managed to feel my way to a large bolster of hay and made myself as comfortable as I could. I had no blankets this time, so I burrowed down into the hay until I was completely wrapped in it like some priceless statue in transit. The Gestapo story stopped me from sleeping very well and there were several occasions when I thought I heard someone walking around outside; each time I looked to see, I found that some cattle had strayed near the barn. It became very cold, lying there in the hay, and the stuff tickled and pricked my skin. Day could not come quickly enough and at 6 o'clock I emerged from my cocoon and stamped up and down the barn to ease the stiffness from my joints. I could not imagine a less prepossessing sight than myself; my clothes were shapeless and studded with hay and I was dirty and unshaven. I was also very hungry as I had missed the 7 o'clock supper (stew), and had had nothing to drink since midday the day before.

Just after 8 the woman called for me, pushing two bikes. 'Ah, you're still here,' she said. 'You must follow me at some distance so that no one thinks that we are together. If you are arrested you must swear—'

'That I don't know you,' I finished.

'Just so,' she said and cycled off at a great pace.

I leapt on my bike and tried to keep her in sight; it was an impossible task. By the time I had reached the top of the first hill she was out of view; either she was a champion cyclist or she knew of a short cut. Anyway, I never saw her again until I reached the outskirts of Mauleon. That I ever did so was remarkably lucky, for time and again I was forced to guess whether to turn right or left. When at length I did overtake my elusive guide she waved me hurriedly past her. As I pedalled, she said, 'Third house on your right.'

It was the last I saw of any of the inhabitants of 'Cold Comfort Farm'. I cannot pretend to be sorry. In many ways it was the most miserable interlude in the whole of our escape.

CHAPTER 15

Awkward Questions

I knocked at the door which the woman had indicated. It was opened by a young woman.

'I am sorry to disturb you,' I said. 'I am looking for a man called L'Allemand. Does he live here?'

From the alarm on the young woman's face when I mentioned the nickname, I knew this must be the right place.

'Why do you want him?' she asked.

I took the risk and told her the truth. She was greatly relieved and invited me inside.

'My husband will be back in about an hour,' she told me. Glad though she was that I was not from the Gestapo, she was still very nervous at having me in the house at all. Any attempt to start a conversation was useless. She was constantly going to the window and peering out at the passers-by, or into the kitchen where she was preparing a meal – but she could not see the road from there and continually popped back into the room where I was sitting in order to do so. By the time L'Allemand returned she was almost in tears.

'There is someone here for you,' I heard her say.

He was very surprised when he saw who it was. I told him what had happened, and he agreed with me that the whole story was almost certainly a fabrication.

'If the Gestapo had been in the area I would know about it,' he said. 'No stranger can pass unnoticed in these parts.'

'I'm glad to have got away,' I told him, 'whatever the reason. By the way, what's the news of Michel? Is he better?'

'Much. They have looked after him very well at the Mouton Blanc and he's been getting up for a few hours every day.'

I was delighted to hear this news, but of course, we were still faced with the problem of where I should stay. L'Allemand did not mention any possibility of my staying with him and his wife, and I did not like to suggest it myself. We had not solved the problem when his wife announced that dinner was ready. There was plenty for the three of us, though I am fairly certain that this was because Madame had quite lost her appetite on account of the strain she had been put under.

'There's only one thing to do,' L'Allemand decided at last, 'and that's for you to go back to the first place you stayed in. They may have a room free by now.'

The only other course was to try to book a room at the hotel with Michel, but for some unknown reason L'Allemand set his face firmly against this idea. Immediately after the meal we set out for the place where we had stayed when we first reached Mauleon. When we arrived, the conversation was carried on entirely in Basque and I could understand none of it; I could pick up enough from the tones and the gestures employed, however, to realize that we were not being enthusiastically received.

'Your old room is free,' L'Allemand told me at last. 'But the trouble is that some people they don't know have written and booked the room next to it and they're due to arrive today. Madame here is convinced that they're members of the Gestapo. Everyone is a bit Gestapo-conscious at the moment – I don't know why.'

'I am quite prepared to pay a bit more to Madame for the trouble which she will be caused by having me on the premises,' I said.

This had the required effect on the family and, after some argument, it was agreed that I should be allowed to stay for two nights. Even now their reluctance to have me was very strong, and I was cut dead by everyone in the house. I stayed in my bedroom and tried to clean myself up a bit. The water was ice cold, but I contrived to have some sort of a shave and wash. With the aid of my hairbrush I was able to remove some of the mud from my suit; in the end, I looked not altogether unpresentable. This improvement in my appearance raised my spirits somewhat, as did a meeting with Michel. He was much better and looked as fit as ever. We were delighted to see each other and he was very amused by my account of my stay at the farm.

'I seem to have had the best end of the bargain after all,' was his comment. 'Still, it's all coming to an end now because I told the proprietor of the hotel that I was only staying on in Mauleon because of my illness. I said that I had come here to see the paintings – and of course the exhibition is over now, so there's no excuse for my staying on now that I'm better.'

'I can't stay in my place either. They aren't at all pleased to see me.'

'It seems to me,' interrupted L'Allemand, 'that the sooner we get going the happier everyone will be.'

Michel and I agreed cordially. It was tedious to be stuck here, waiting to take the last hurdle.

'I will go and see the guide tonight,' L'Allemand went on, 'and see what can be arranged. I'll see you tomorrow morning.'

He shook hands with us and went off on his way. Michel and I went for a walk, partly to test his newly regained strength, partly to make some purchases for our journey. We each bought a knapsack which would be easier to manage over the mountains than the battered suitcases we had used until now. I also bought a pair of espadrilles, canvas shoes with thick rubber soles. We dined together at the Mouton Blanc and agreed to meet there again the next morning.

We were just beginning our breakfast when L'Allemand came in.

'I've seen the guide,' he said, 'and I've managed to persuade him to make an attempt to get off tonight.'

'That's wonderful,' cried Michel.

'We'll see,' was the cautious reply. 'Conditions are far from perfect, but we can't expect the weather to last much longer so they're probably the best we can hope for. The top surface should be pretty hard by now. There's a fair chance we'll get through.'

'I suppose we shall have to go as we are,' I said.

'Your clothes don't matter too much,' L'Allemand told us. 'Your shoes are the main trouble. I don't think there's a hope of getting you any spiked boots. There's only one shop where you might be able to get some – if you were prepared to pay for them.'

'We could pay for them all right.'

'That may be, but I don't know the proprietor of the shop. He's a new man. There are no mountains where you could possibly need to use climbing boots except those between us and Spain. And I'm not too keen on anyone knowing that you're thinking about that particular climb!'

We decided that we would make do with our own shoes. Then we went up to Michel's bedroom where L'Allemand gave us precise instructions with the help of a large survey map of the area.

Michel and I had an early lunch at the hotel, then we went round to where I was staying to pack up my things and wait for L'Allemand. Madame became quite affable when she heard that I was leaving and insisted on presenting me with a large fruit cake which she had baked only that morning. The day was bright and sunny and augured well for our climb, yet in spite of the sun the temperature was well below freezing.

L'Allemand brought two bicycles round to my place just after 2 o'clock. At 4.30 he returned to collect us – and the final stage of our Odyssey began.

L'Allemand and I cycled out of Mauleon in one direction while Michel, according to plan, took another road which would enable him to meet us a few kilometres out of the village. The sun was already sinking and hung like a vivid red ball in the lowering mist. L'Allemand and I had cycled perhaps a mile without encountering anyone when, rounding a bend, we suddenly saw three French customs officers right in our path. Their bikes were stacked at the side of the road and they were standing watching the sunset and having a smoke; their rifles were slung over their shoulders. They turned and watched as we came towards them and we knew that we would have to cycle on past them; it was too late to turn back. We rode slowly as if there was no particular object in our little jaunt. For a mere moment I thought they were going to let us pass, but as we came abreast of them their sergeant held out his hand and called out, 'Just a minute.'

We stopped our bikes.

'Good evening,' said L'Allemand.

'Good evening, gentlemen. May I enquire where you are going on this lovely winter evening?'

The two other officials closed round us.

'We're not going anywhere,' I told him. 'We're just taking the air before supper.'

'Really? I should have thought it was the sort of evening when one would prefer to stay by one's fire. Still, as you like the cold countryside so much that you have to go riding about on a bike, I suppose you have a licence to do so?'

L'Allemand produced his.

'I'm afraid I seem to have left mine behind,' I said lamely.

'Oh, I am sorry to hear that, Monsieur, really. I'm afraid that will cost you a hundred francs.' He drew out a small pad and a butt end of pencil. 'Now then, just a few details, if you please. Your name?' I told him my present name. 'Your address?'

'Sixteen Rue de Pigalle.'

'Where are you staying in Mauleon?'

'At the Mouton Blanc,' I said.

'Oh, not far away,' was his comment. 'We shall easily be able to check on that. And whose bicycle is that you are riding?'

'I borrowed it from my friend here,' I said, pointing to L'Allemand. I only hoped that he would not ask me what my friend's name was because I knew him only by his nickname.

'You're quite sure you didn't steal it?'

'Really, what do you take me for?'

'We will see. Well, here is the receipt for your hundred francs,' he said, tearing off the stub of paper from his pad.

'Thank you,' I said with what I hoped was dignity. We prepared to remount our bikes.

'Just a moment, if you don't mind. Would I be indiscreet in asking you gentlemen for your papers?'

He only glanced at L'Allemand's and handed it back to him. But when he took mine I could see that we were in for a long session.

'You are from Paris, I see.'

'I told you so before,' I replied coldly.

'Of course. What was the address again?'

'Sixteen Rue de Pigalle.'

'Lived there long?'

'I was born there.'

'Really? What was your father's name?'

'Gaston.'

'Your mother's?'

'Yvonne.'

'What was your father's occupation?'

'Engineer.'

'How many brothers did you have?'

'Three.'

'Sisters?'

'Two.'

'What was your eldest brother's name?'

'Jean.'

'The youngest?'

'Henri.'

'How old is your youngest sister?'

'Um – nineteen.'

'Her name?'

'Thérèse.'

'Is your oldest brother older than your oldest sister?'

'Yes.'

'How much?'

'Five years.'

'Do you live in a house or a flat?'

'A flat.'

'What buses pass the door?'

'Er – the forty-five and the ninety-one.'

'The nearest Métro?'

'Montmartre.'

'What is your oldest sister's name?'

'Marthe.'

'And how many sisters do you have?'

'Three.'

'And brothers?'

'Three – er – that is, two.'

'Really? You surprise me. What is your youngest brother's name?'

'Gaston.'

'Oh, excuse me, I thought that was the eldest.'

'Oh, no – the eldest is . . . um . . .'

'It is difficult to remember one's brother's name, isn't it?'

'Paul,' I said.

'Of course! Did you say you lived at number fourteen Rue de Pigalle?'

'Eighteen,' I corrected him.

'Or was it sixteen?'

'Never,' I said, blushing fiercely.

'You will forgive me saying so, I'm sure, but you seem somewhat flustered. Is something wrong?'

'Certainly not.'

'May I see your *carte de travail?*'

I handed it to him, cursing that I had not taken the trouble to decipher the name of the firm I was supposed to be working for. He stared at the *carte* for a while and then asked the obvious question.

'What is the name of the firm for which you work, and what is their address?'

'As you can read all the particulars off the card you have in your hand, I don't see why you have to ask me,' I said angrily.

'You mean,' he said, smiling blandly, 'that my guess is as good as yours!' He handed the card back to me. 'May I see what you have in your knapsack?'

I took it from my back and gave it to him. I was almost past caring now, waiting only for the dismal farce to end. I knew he knew, and he knew I knew he knew. He was now playing for laughs.

'Well, well,' he cried as he opened the sack, 'what have we here? I thought you said you were just taking the air before supper. Do you always take your pyjamas and your toothbrush and your razor and a new pair of espadrilles when going on such a ride? You know, if I were a suspicious sort of person, I should think you were setting out on a little trip.'

I gave up any attempt to reply. It was hopeless and I knew it. We could not fight our way out against three armed men and certainly we had failed to bluff our way out. We might be able to make a run for it on the way back to Mauleon, but at the moment there was nothing to be done. I glanced at L'Allemand, looking for some sort of inspiration; he was staring at his feet, utterly dejected. The only thing that occurred to me was that these men were, after all, Frenchmen. Perhaps some kind of emotional appeal? Or would a bribe be more realistic?

The sergeant was putting the things back in my knapsack. He handed it to me with a smile – a full, broad smile this time – and his eyes were sparkling with amusement.

'Hop it,' he said. 'Hop it quick! And remember: we never met. The best of luck!'

I stood and stared at him. I have never been so surprised. I could not believe he meant it. I did not move. Were they intending to shoot us as we 'attempted to escape'?

'Hop it, man, and make it snappy. Or would you rather I arrested you?'

I slung my knapsack on my back and leapt on to my bike.

L'Allemand and I pedalled off as fast as we could go. A voice behind us called out, 'Thanks for the hundred francs.'

When we had safely rounded the next bend I glanced at L'Allemand and said, 'That was a bit too close for my taste.'

To my astonishment L'Allemand was grinning all over his face.

'You were superb,' he told me.

'What do you mean?'

'Well, these French guards are generally good chaps and they help us whenever they can, but their great fear is that the Boche will set a trap for them just to check that they do their job. Well, anyone could tell after two minutes that you couldn't be a trap. The more tied up you got the better it was. As soon as he opened your knapsack I knew we were all right. No one could have had a less plausible story than you!'

'Thank you,' I said.

We were cycling along at a fair pace in an effort to make up for the time we had lost. As we came round a shallow bend in the road we saw three men cycling ahead of us in the gloom.

'Germans,' said L'Allemand.

We dismounted and flung ourselves and our machines into the ditch. We lay there flat to the ground for five minutes, waiting for the sound of the Germans returning to investigate. But they did not come.

'This is all a bit much,' L'Allemand decided. 'I think we'd better ditch the bikes and proceed on foot. We're fairly close to the place where we're meeting Michel, and we can take a short cut across the fields.'

We did as L'Allemand suggested and soon arrived at the barn where Michel was waiting for us. He had had no trouble in getting there and had met no one on the road. We hid Michel's bike in the barn and followed L'Allemand down a rough track. After an hour's march we picked up the first guide, who was introduced to us as Jean.

'Please follow in single file,' he told us, 'and make as little noise as possible. When I do this with my hand I want you to stand stock-still. I shall go ahead to spy out the land. And, please, no talking or smoking.'

For the first hour the going was fairly easy and the ground more or less level. Then the climb began. From 6 to 7 o'clock we climbed steadily, sometimes along a track, at others across rough ground. It grew very dark, the man ahead a mere shadow, and loose stones underfoot made the going difficult. Most of the country was wooded and as we climbed higher patches of ice and snow began to appear like luminous islands in the darkness. The temperature must have fallen to 10 or 12 degrees below zero, but the exertion of our walk kept us warm.

Just after 7 we halted for ten minutes while the guide and L'Allemand went forward to see whether it was safe for us to enter a small village two or three hundred yards ahead. We had to cross a fairly wide torrent and the only bridge was situated in the village. Michel and I ate a couple of hunks of fruit cake.

'All clear,' whispered L'Allemand as they returned. Soon we had crossed the bridge and were climbing again. The moon came up and relieved the sombre gloom of our progress; we could now see very clearly. The higher we climbed the rougher the ground became; the ice was no longer in patches, it stretched unendingly ahead. Then the woods ended. We were now in a field of ice where it became very hard to keep one's footing; I was wearing leather soles and could hardly stand up at all. I spent much of my time on all-fours. Jean and L'Allemand strode on ahead, their spiked boots biting crisply into the ice.

'Come on, keep up,' Jean called impatiently.

They had to keep coming back and helping me to my feet and Jean grew more and more impatient. Finally he stopped and called us together.

'We must go faster,' he told us. 'We're half an hour behind schedule already; we'll never make the rendezvous with our next guide unless we crack up the pace. We have to go fast now because conditions get a great deal worse later on. Now for God's sake keep—'

'It's not my fault,' I said, 'it's these shoes. I can't stop myself slipping.'

'Isn't there something you can tie round them – rope or canvas or something?'

'I'd quite forgotten,' I exclaimed. 'I've got a pair of espadrilles in my sack. They might do the trick.'

'Try them – and be quick about it.'

I hurriedly changed and found that my grip on the ice was much improved. We pressed on. The pace was faster now and Michel and I got sorely out of breath on some of the steeper bits. Jean and L'Allemand strode on firmly; both were young men and they had lived all their lives in the mountains. Even after his illness Michel was standing the pace better than I; he was a good deal younger and better equipped physically. Thirty-five is a bit late in the day for a man to start walking up mountains, particularly if he has been smoking about forty cigarettes a day for the past six months.

We tramped and tramped through the ice-field, never a pause, never a rest. When I thought I could stand no more and must beg for a rest we topped a crest and started to descend. I just managed to get my breath back.

A strong wind was now blowing from the north-east and Michel and I began to feel the cold for the first time. We reached and crossed a pine wood and then started to climb again. Soon we came to a large barn.

'Wait in here,' Jean ordered, opening the door. 'I'm going to see a friend of mine who can tell me what conditions are like on the mountains. It may not be worthwhile going on.'

The barn was full of sheep which were sheltering there for the night; however, the shelter was not as good as it might have been and icy draughts whipped through the broken and rotted slats of the barn walls. By the end of an hour we were shivering with cold. The snow on my canvas shoes (which had melted as I walked) had now frozen into ice. Both my feet were completely numb. At last Jean came back.

'Conditions are far from good,' he reported. 'Some of the drifts are several feet thick and the top surface, although it's frozen all right, isn't very thick. I don't know that it'll hold us. What do you want to do?'

'Go on,' L'Allemand said, and we supported him.

'All right. We should be at the next guide's hut at one-thirty. We can get a hot meal there and have a good long rest.'

Once more we set off. We were all a bit stiff after our long wait and my feet were like two blocks of wood, heavy and without feeling. For the first half-hour the going was quite easy and we were able to loosen up; there were plenty of trees again and the footing was firm. Then the trees ended and again we were on a surface of frozen snow. Every now and then this would give way under us and we would sink in up to the ankle or the knee, sometimes even as far as the waist. Jean looked back anxiously.

'I don't like it,' he said. 'Just look at those tracks.'

We turned and looked. All along the path we had followed were little pits where we had sunk in. They showed like craters in the moonlight.

'You couldn't miss those,' Michel muttered.

'If the frontier guards spot them they'll be on us like knives.'

I thought of the Alsatians I had seen in Pau. 'Like wolves,' I murmured.

Jean led on and the path levelled out. On all sides the frozen snow glittered with light under the moon as we walked on. Now we were passing along the side of a mountain and, to the left, the ground fell away steeply to the dark valley below. Beyond the black pit of the valley was a barrier of great white peaks. We tramped on, up and up, for two hours. Nobody spoke. The barrier of mountains stood endless against the backdrop of the sky. At last we topped the ridge and began the slow descent. The snow was very deep in places; several times one of us sank into it up to his armpits. As we got lower conditions improved, and at last we reached the shelter of some trees where the going was much easier. It was now after 1 o'clock and I was dead beat; I walked on automatically, as I had done for the last eight hours. I was buoyed up by the thought that the worst was over and that we should soon be able to relax and get a good meal and a long sleep. We plodded forward.

It was just on 2 when we reached the guide's log hut. He was fast asleep and we had quite a job to rouse him, but at last he let us in. The embers of a log fire were smouldering in the grate and he flung some more pieces of wood on it. Soon it blazed up comfortingly. Jean and our new host carried on a long conversation which, since it was all in Basque, we could not understand. Michel and I flopped down by the fire and soon were almost asleep.

At length the buzz of conversation ceased; evidently a decision of some kind had been reached.

'Please listen to me,' Jean called. Michel and I sat up. 'We must continue our journey at once.' I could not believe it.

'There have been a number of patrols in this area,' cut in the second guide. 'One of them might call here at any time, so we must go on. If they pick up your tracks anywhere along the route you've taken, that will lead them straight here. Come on, we must go.'

'I can't,' I pleaded. 'I know I can't make it without a long rest.'

'What do you think?' L'Allemand enquired of the two guides.

'The Germans have trebled their patrols in the last few weeks. A lot of POWs have been getting out this way and they're trying to stop them,' the second guide explained. 'We must leave immediately.'

'I shall only hold you up,' I said. 'That's what's worrying me.'

'I will carry your knapsack for you,' the second guide said. 'And I promise we will not go too fast.'

As he spoke he was getting wine, bread and cheese from a cupboard; he put these on the table and we sat down to eat. While we ate he got ready for the climb. The food made me feel a bit better, but both Michel and I were still very cold. My hands were stiff and swollen, and I could still feel nothing in my feet at all.

'Now we must go,' the guide said.

We shook Jean by the hand and thanked him for his help. As we set off towards the south we saw him begin his journey back towards the north.

We waved once and then the trek began again.

It was like walking in broad daylight, so bright was the moon and so clear the atmosphere.

'It's too clear for my liking,' said the guide. 'Once we get out on the snow they'll be able to see us miles away.'

The first hour was easy; the track ran downwards through more pine woods and the only obstacles were small torrents which we had to negotiate with the help of rather poor and submerged stepping-stones. Then we started to climb again. As we did so, the guide came back and gave me his alpenstock to help me on my way; this coupled with his carrying my knapsack was a great kindness and made the climb a deal less trying, at least for a while.

The rough track which we had been following disappeared and yet the guide forged steadily forward, never faltering. We were now hugging the side of the mountain we eventually had to cross. The going grew steeper all the time. The side of the mountain fell away to our left and the course we were taking took us diagonally across it. Again, in spite of the espadrilles, I found it very tough to keep my footing; I kept slipping away down the slope. It was impossible to press on at all now without resting, and the guide allowed us a few minutes in each half hour to get our breath. Then we would push forward again, resuming the relentless plod.

At 4.30 we reached the summit of the first peak and started down the other side. At this point we actually crossed into Spain – but an hour later we crossed back into France. On and on we went, down the sheer side of the mountain. At one of our halts the guide called us together and pointed to a towering peak over to the left which soared into the sky like a shimmering giant.

'That's our last obstacle,' he told us. 'Once we get over that little fellow it's downhill all the way into Spain.'

I looked at the great mountain and knew I should never make it. Only the hope which Spain provided gave me what little courage I managed to muster.

'There's a log hut just over the top,' the guide went on, 'and we can rest there. Take a quarter of an hour's break now. Once we start there'll be no stopping. Day is just dawning, and once it comes we shall be visible for miles and we'll have to make all the speed we can. Apart from that, it'll be very cold and windy when we get near the summit and if you stop you will never start again.'

As he spoke the first rays of the sun came glancing off the peaks like a million swords. Michel and I stood and tried to get our breath controlled and easy.

'Forward,' said the guide, all too soon it seemed.

We began the last lap.

CHAPTER 16

Over the Mountain

We seemed to have been climbing through all eternity. I had no idea how long it was since the guide had cried 'Forward' and we had begun the long toiling ascent. Whenever a twist in our path brought us in view of the summit it still stood as impregnable, as aloof and as inaccessible as before. The galling cold grew more intense. Still we continued to climb and the breath in my lungs was as heavy as stone. I could hear the thumping of my heart. Strange black shapes flitted across my eyes.

At times we had to proceed on all-fours while the guide cut steps for us in the ice. My lungs felt as if they would burst, as if they were full and could not admit any more air. The saliva was frozen on my lips. Now I no longer looked up to see how close we were to the peak; my head was sunk down watching the weary plodding of my feet. I was sure that each step would be my last, that I should drop down in sheer exhaustion, but even as my body demanded rest it surprised me by its ability to continue without a pause. I was moving step by step now. Was it will-power or mere physical habit that kept me going? I really cannot tell, but I do know that I kept moving upwards and upwards. I could not tell now whether the sun was bright or not; the light kept fading and I thought I was near to a blackout. The breath was rasping in my throat as I gulped for oxygen. I could not go on. On we went. If I fell I would never get up. I kept staggering forward.

The guide stopped. Hardly conscious, I was vaguely able to appreciate that we were on a fairly level patch of ice. There was thick mist up here and it was snowing heavily. I had not realized it until then; no wonder I had not been able to see too well. I leaned heavily on my alpenstock and tried to get my breath, the fat snowflakes falling against my lips. The guide was talking.

'Up here,' he shouted, pointing to our right, 'and we're at the top. From there it's plain sailing.'

I looked up to where he had pointed. A sheer wall of ice, absolutely smooth, rose up into the mist and vanished. The top was at least a hundred feet up this cliff.

'You can rest at the top,' the guide was saying, 'if we can get into the hut. Now keep close behind me and put your toes carefully into the niches I cut in the ice. If you slip, God knows how far you'll fall.'

The guide went first, I came next, followed by Michel and L'Allemand. I tried to keep calm and to conserve my last remaining energy for when I should really need it. The ascent was desperately slow. The wind tore at us as if to rend us from our perilous perch, and the snow had now turned to fierce pebbles of hail. I could see only a few yards in the mist and I waited, peering upwards, for when the guide should have cut the next niche. He did this by kicking at the ice with the toe of his boot; he was very sure-footed and what was a foothold for him was not always one for me; often I had to kick at the ice myself in order to enlarge the niche. I felt no pain when I did this, though I was still wearing only the thin canvas espadrilles which I had changed into on the lower slopes. I had felt nothing at all in my feet since we left the barn with the sheep in it.

The wind almost dragged me away from the wall of ice. I had to use all my remaining strength to stop myself from falling, and as I used it I knew that I should not be able to go much farther. I could not tell whether my fingers were in the hand-holds or not; it seemed that I was hanging without support in mid-air. I flattened myself against the wall. The guide had vanished into the mist above me now and I was stuck there like a fly on a paper, unable to move up or down. I was quite alone. The others had left me. I started up the slope again, but now I could not find the holes which the guide had kicked; I had to kick new ones for myself, stabbing at the hard ice in my canvas shoes, stubbing my unfeeling toes against it. Then I stopped. I could never start again of my own accord. I knew I should just hang there until I dropped off through complete exhaustion. I felt a cruel sob of utter despair run through my body like a fever.

A strong arm circled round me from below and Michel's voice shouted close in my ear, 'Go on, *mon vieux*, we're there!' I struggled up another few yards and was again at my last gasp when another pair of arms reached down from above and caught me under the armpits; I was dragged up those last few feet and on to the ledge, where I passed out completely.

I woke to find neat gin being forced down my throat. I shook my head, gulped a little more gin and then hauled myself up on to my feet. Michel and the guide helped me forward and we rounded a spur of snow which afforded us some protection from the wind and the hail. We stood there together, breathing in the air which we felt we had been lacking for a long time. After a few minutes the sun slanted through the clouds and the mist, leaving the sky clear and bright.

The knowledge that the worst was really over encouraged me to make another effort to go on.

'Are you ready now?' the guide asked gently.

'Ready,' I said.

My legs and knees were very stiff and my progress very slow; it was not made any easier by the softness of the snow. There had been a fairly heavy fall during the night which had not yet had time to harden. At each step we sank in several inches, and we had to expend a lot of extra energy dragging our way through the drifts. We had been walking for seventeen hours . . .

The sun now shone very brightly and the glare of its rays on the snow was almost blinding. We plodded on for about half an hour and then, a few hundred feet below us and down to our right, we saw the roof of the log hut.

'You wait here,' the guide told us. 'I'll go forward and check that all is well.'

Soon he was waving us on. We reached the hut and went in. Inside there were two double bunks, a wooden table, a few stools and an iron stove. A pile of logs was heaped against one wall. The windows were covered with heavy wooden shutters and it was very dark as a result.

'We shan't be staying here long enough for it to be worth lighting a fire,' the guide said. 'We'll just have a quick snack and then press on. We've still got about three hours' march ahead of us before we reach the frontier, I'm afraid.'

L'Allemand unpacked his knapsack and took out some thickly cut meat sandwiches. We tucked in eagerly. Michel and I shared out the remains of our fruit cake, and we washed the whole lot down with gulps of neat gin. I could hardly keep awake now; after all, I had been without sleep for twenty-four hours.

I couldn't help being amused at the difference between L'Allemand and our guide on the one hand, and Michel and myself on the other. They were as fresh as if they had not yet started out and their warm woollen lumber-jackets, Balaclava helmets, heavy boots and thick socks made them look very much at home in the surroundings in which we found ourselves. They were chatting away in Basque, quite untired and unmarked by the climb. Michel and I, however, were not in such good shape. We looked ludicrously incongruous in our city clothes to begin with; in addition we were both at the point of collapse, though Michel had stood the pace wonderfully well and, in spite of his recent attack of flu, never once complained.

'I think we ought to get going again,' I suggested after a while. It may seem strange that it was I who made the suggestion that we should go on, but I felt that if we stayed much longer I would just fall asleep and probably not wake for hours. Also, I could feel my joints beginning to stiffen and already I knew it would take several minutes of exercise before I could get on the move again. As I slowly rose to my feet I found I could scarcely keep my balance; I had to hang on to the table to stay upright. When we were outside I felt very thirsty, and I was about to put some snow in my mouth to melt it when the guide stopped me.

'You'll get cramp in your stomach that way,' he warned me. As I had guessed, the half-hour in the hut had, if anything, worsened my condition by allowing me to relax. I kept almost falling asleep, and somehow I could not take the march seriously; I could not settle down to it again. I floundered forward, uncontrolled and uncaring. I could not move my eyes; I just stared at the ground a few feet ahead of me. Now I had no idea how long it was since we had left the hut. I was neither hot nor cold. I hardly felt I existed.

The newly fallen snow afforded a fairly good surface to walk on; although it was tiring it was at least safe. Now, however, the snow disappeared (we had been descending for some time) and we emerged again on to ice. The sun beat down on the white surface as I stumbled on. Suddenly, without warning, the ice gave way; I tipped up, my left leg sinking in right up to the thigh. I had no strength to pull myself out. When Michel came to help me, he too fell through. Nevertheless he managed to support me and we crawled forward on all-fours back to the safer ice. I could hardly drag myself back on to my feet after this accident, and for the next twenty minutes it was repeated again and again. I was so weak now that every time I tripped I fell full length and the pain of continuing was the greater each time. I hardly wanted to continue; I wanted to sleep, just sleep.

At last we came to a stronger plain of ice and I was able to carry on with less difficulty, though from time to time I had blackouts. The man in front of me stopped. I stopped.

'We are now in Spain,' the guide said. 'We'll rest here for a few moments and then tackle the last little bit.'

I must have fallen asleep where I stood, for the next thing I knew someone was rubbing snow over my face and neck; this woke me up a little. The guide passed me the gin bottle and I took a long swig. My head cleared slightly. I was able to see that we were now down in the valley; there were trees by the side of a small torrent which, the guide explained, ran all the way to the inn which was our final destination.

'How long?' I mumbled.

'Two hours.'

'How long since we were at the hut?'

'Three hours.'

'One last effort, old man,' whispered Michel.

I staggered forward a few paces and collapsed on the ice. Michel and the others helped me up. I staggered forward a few more paces and went down again. The gin bottle was put to my lips and I was pulled to my feet. Again I stumbled a few steps on and passed out. Again they raised me. And so it continued, with me almost unconscious, for three hours till at last we reached the haven of the inn. Our twenty-three-hour trip was ended.

When finally I came to myself, I found I was sitting in front of a huge log fire in a long, low, whitewashed room. Michel was sitting beside me and I grinned at him dopily. Someone handed me a large bowl of hot soup and after a few sips I was able to take in what was going on around me. In addition to my three companions there were seven or eight other people in the room.

'Who are they?' I whispered to Michel.

'French men and women. They crossed into Spain – by a shorter way than ours – a few days ago. They haven't been able to get any farther than this because of the weather, but they're hoping to move on tomorrow. We might go with them.'

The innkeeper and his wife came up and were introduced to me. They seemed very kind and said that I was to ask for anything I wanted. Sleep was the thing I wanted most and soon Madame took me up to our bedroom which the four of us were to share. It contained two single beds and Michel and I had to share one of them. I shed some of my clothing and removed my espadrilles. In spite of the heat of the fire downstairs I found that the lower parts of both my trouser legs were still frozen stiff as drainpipes. I threw myself into bed and fell asleep at once.

I woke in agony. My feet felt as though they were clamped in a slowly closing vice. I threw back the blankets, and with a shock I saw that my feet were swollen up to nearly twice their normal size and the socks which contained them (I had not removed them before going to bed) were stretched to bursting point. I removed them now and looked at my feet. They need washing, I thought; they were quite black in fact. When I swung them round towards the window (it was still daylight) to get a better view of them, I saw that it was not dirt which made them black, or rather a deep purple, but frostbite. There could be no doubt about that.

I remembered that I had heard one should rub a frost-bitten area with snow and thought of struggling downstairs to get some. In the end, however, I knew I could not get there so instead I reached for one of my shoes and banged it on the floor. It took a lot of banging to attract attention, but at last Michel came running up the stairs.

'Hullo,' he said, 'I never thought to see you awake for at least two days!'

'If it weren't for my feet,' I replied, 'you wouldn't have done.' When he saw their condition he hurried off and fetched the innkeeper and his wife. They conferred for a minute and then said that it was definitely frostbite but that it was far too late for rubbing in snow. I should have to see a doctor. The nearest one lived seven or eight hours away in a village called Orbiseta.

Meanwhile the innkeeper's wife brought some olive oil with which she bathed my feet, bandaging them up with lint.

L'Allemand and the other guide came into the room, both very concerned about me and deploring my bad luck. The innkeeper said that he could go and see a neighbour of his who might be able to lend one of his mules for me to ride to the doctor's. Luckily we had enough Spanish money to make it likely that he would agree to the loan. There was no chance of going until the next morning, so until then they would make me as comfortable as they could.

Michel came to bed very early and, though the bed was very narrow, neither of us had any difficulty in getting a good night's rest. We were awakened at 6 a.m. the next morning when the guide and L'Allemand got up. They went downstairs to breakfast and returned afterwards to say goodbye before starting the long trek home.

'Before you go,' Michel said, 'we have something for you.' So saying, he handed them all the remaining French banknotes which we still had. They were useless to us now and, furthermore, it was a punishable offence to bring them into Spain. It was small recompense for what the two of them had done for us.

Next, to my intense embarrassment and Michel's delight, the two of them sprang to attention, saluted and then, in turn, came forward and kissed me soundly on both cheeks.

'*Bon voyage et bonne chance, mon capitaine,*' they said.

They shook Michel warmly by the hand and were gone. So ended our last link with the escape line. I found out later that we were the last two people to travel by it; it was 'blown' shortly afterwards, but fortunately sufficient warning was received and few arrests were made. Our Paris contact managed to cross into Spain and make her way to England where I met her again. François, L'Allemand and the guide also crossed into Spain and remained there, until just before D-Day; then they went back into France and joined the Maquis.

My feet proved to be very troublesome and I had to spend a good many weeks in various Spanish hospitals before I knew for certain that I would not have to have both of them amputated. As it was, I lost the big toe of my left foot and all but the middle toe of my right; I was lucky to come out so well, and would not have done so were it not for the kindness of the Spaniards and the skill of the surgeon who operated on me in Madrid. I must also record here the kindness of the Embassy staff in Madrid who loaded me with gifts, and who arranged for me to have books and visitors. I had been separated from Michel for a long time, as he was confined in a concentration camp at Miranda until the British Embassy managed to secure his release. He was with me for a week in Madrid and then he went on to Gibraltar. It was some time before I was able to follow him.

On 5 June 1944, I finally landed in England; it was the day before

D-Day. That night, among other messages which must have given the word to a thousand Resistance organizations that the great day was at hand, a personal message went out from London on the French Service of the B.B.C.: '*Le Sanglier et le Chat Sauvage seront toujours bons amis.*'

It was over.